The
10 %
Solution

Your Key to Financial Security

THIS BOOK IS DEDICATED TO . . .

My grandmother, Fannie
My mother, Sylvia
My father, Irving
My children, Alan and Jill

The 10 % Solution

Your Key to Financial Security

Ed Blitz

LIBERTY HOUSE®

LIBERTY HOUSE books are published by LIBERTY HOUSE, a division of TAB BOOKS Inc. Its trademark, consisting of the words "LIBERTY HOUSE" and the portrayal of Benjamin Franklin, is registered in the United States Patent and Copyright Office.

FIRST EDITION
FIRST PRINTING

Library of Congress Cataloging in Publication Data

Blitz, Ed.
The 10% solution : your key to financial security / by
Ed Blitz.
p. cm.
Includes index.
ISBN 0-8306-3023-6 (pbk.)
1. Finance, Personal. I. Title. II. Title: Ten percent
solution.
HG179.B556 1988
332.024—dc19   88-16978
                                                CIP

TAB BOOKS Inc. offers software for
sale. For information and a catalog,
please contact TAB Software Department,
Blue Ridge Summit, PA 17294-0850.

Questions regarding the content of this book
should be addressed to:

Reader Inquiry Branch
TAB BOOKS Inc.
Blue Ridge Summit, PA 17294-0214

Contents

Acknowledgments

I HAVE BEEN FORTUNATE TO RECEIVE THE SUPPORT OF MANY IN MY WRITING.

I would like to thank my parents, my children and Marilyn, for their love and belief in me, without which this book would never have been written.

Thanks too, to my fans, Betty and Sam Siklek, for watching all of the TV shows and reading everything that I wrote.

Thanks are also due my friends and associates, Tony Attanasio, Mike Lee, and Anne Breight, for putting up with this project and the distractions it caused.

I am grateful, too, to Virginia Webster for her typing, to Bill Gladstone, my agent, and to Ellie Robotta and Brenda Gilmore for their encouragement.

And special thanks to my friend, Sue Strom, for believing in the book and being instrumental in its publication.

Saving—making money faster than your family can spend it.

Introduction

THIS BOOK WILL PROVIDE YOU WITH A REVIEW OF YOUR CURRENT FINANCIAL situation, and recommendations to meet specific financial objectives and improve your overall financial condition.

The most important concept to be learned from this book is very simple—*10% Off the Top*. From now on, 10% of everything you ever earn or receive should be set aside for growth, for investment, for savings—*for you*!

Don't let *10% Off the Top* scare you. It is a goal! If it is impossible for you to start at this level try 5%, 1%, or even ½%. You need to start somewhere. As your financial situation improves, you can increase your savings percentage toward the goal of 10%.

It may be hard to imagine taking a percentage out of your income for savings. However, once you get in the habit, it will become as natural as paying your telephone bill. Start with 10% the first month and see if you can make it through. If it is impossible, try 7% or 5%. If that is impossible try 1% or ½% at an absolute minimum. After you have gone over the budgeting exercise in Chapter 4, review the nonessentials in your budget, and try to reduce those to accommodate your savings. This effort—the reduction of some of your "luxuries"—will pay off in a big way. Make every attempt to set a savings goal of *10% Off the Top* but, again, if it is impossible, start with a lesser goal and work your way up.

Reference will be made to *10% Off the Top* throughout the book. If you are starting at a lower level, just assume that the reference is a reminder to you at your current savings level.

There are two basic objectives of financial planning:

- To increase real after-tax cash flow or spendable income

- To increase wealth accumulation or asset growth

By following the guidelines and suggestions in this book, you will be well on your way to achieving these two goals.

Read this book several times, complete the various worksheets, follow the suggestions made, and always save *10% Off the Top*.

Make no little plans. They have no magic to stir men's blood.
Make big plans. Aim high in hope and work.—*D. H. Burnham*

1

Your Financial Plan

The Goal: Financial Well-Being

BEFORE GETTING INTO THE VARIOUS ASPECTS OF YOUR FINANCIAL PLAN MAKE
the following commitment right here and now:

> **I, _____, will set aside 10% (or ___ %) of every dollar
> I earn or receive from today on.**

If you make and keep this commitment, I promise that you will not only be
on your way to becoming a much wealthier person, but it will be one of the easiest things you have ever done.

Though you may have never thought about or understood financial planning,
though you may have the erroneous notion that financial planning is for the su-
perwealthy, though you may have not succeeded with past investments, make
this commitment and follow it without deviation.

Begin by simply opening a new savings account at your most convenient bank,
preferably the same one where you cash or deposit your paychecks. I don't care
how many savings accounts you may already have, I want you to open a new
one. Try to get the highest-rate account possible, but don't worry too much about
that now. More importantly, *open that account.*

The next time you receive a paycheck, simply take 10% of the amount of
the check, deposit it into this new account, and do whatever you wish (or normally do) with the remainder. Later we will review various strategies, budgets,

1

and so on. But for now, put that 10% to work for you. Remember, every time you get paid, whether weekly, semi-monthly, monthly, or whatever, 10% goes into this new account. If you receive a bonus, interest, dividends, or even a gift, 10% of that goes into the account as well.

Even if the 10% is only $1.10, I want you to make that deposit. The purpose of this is to provide you with a means of becoming extremely wealthy. Otherwise, you will always spend all you make, and you will probably try to spend more than you make.

Don't be misled into believing that you will save the excess of your income over your expenses—you will find some way to spend it. You will come up with lots of reasons why you can't save money, or why you must spend it. But from today on, you have committed to a new "expense," *10% Off the Top*. You will only achieve this financial independence and wealth if you make this commitment and take the money out of reach so that it appears to be spent. You will achieve wealth only by making it a part of what you spend!

For the time being, just keep depositing that *10% Off the Top*. As you are introduced to the various ideas presented in this book, you may wish to put some or all of this accumulated savings elsewhere, but for now, don't worry about other types of investments.

Now let's go into other areas of your financial plan. We'll get back to your accumulated savings later.

Your financial plan will have the following elements, in the following order of priority:

- Basic needs: To provide adequately for current living expenses (food, clothing, shelter, etc.)

- Insurance: To provide resources in the event of catastrophe (death, disability, unforeseen expenses)

- Educational needs: To provide for the education of your children

- Wealth accumulation and retirement needs: To provide financial independence and adequate reserves for retirement

- Asset growth: To use good principles of investment to ensure the growth of assets and to keep risk to a minimum

- Income tax planning: To keep income taxes to their lowest levels

- Estate planning: To keep estate taxes to a minimum, to provide liquidity, and to preserve and direct the disposition of assets to heirs

The questions you need to ask yourself are the following (be honest when you answer):

- How do my living expenses compare to my income?
- If there is an emergency, do I have a cash reserve or other assets that can easily be sold or converted into cash?
- If I am injured or die suddenly, do I have enough insurance to continue to provide for my family?
- Can I pay for my children's education?
- Can I retire comfortably?
- Have I taken advantage of all potential tax savings?
- Do I have a good mix of investments, or are "all my eggs in one basket"?

If you are not satisfied with all your answers, read on, and don't forget the *10% Off the Top.*

Paper Clip: A product used as a pipecleaner, radio connection, garter clasp, toothpick, necktie clasp, costume jewelry, for twisting when nervous, and sometimes even for clipping a few papers together.

2

Recordkeeping

Getting Organized

MAINTAINING ORGANIZED RECORDS OF YOUR ASSETS AND LIABILITIES IS IMPORTANT in financial planning. It will also allow for a smooth transition in the case of death or illness. Without organized records, considerable time and expense can be involved in settling your estate.

There are many systems to use for the organization of records. As long as a system works for you, it is acceptable. Step back and review your system by asking yourself: Can anyone take my records and immediately and easily determine what assets, debts, and insurance policies I have? If the answer is yes, then you have an excellent recordkeeping system.

Photocopy FIGS. 2-1A/B through 2-7A/B for your use in reviewing all of your assets, liabilities, etc. These worksheets should be kept with a copy of your will and trust documents in a place where they can be easily found. Review and update these records at least annually.

RETENTION OF RECORDS

One of the most frequently asked questions is: How long do I have to keep copies of my tax returns or other documents?

Generally, records such as tax returns should be kept for a minimum of 6 to 7 years. Records pertaining to the purchase of a home or other major assets should be kept for a longer period.

Recently, the American Institute of Certified Public Accountants, in conjunction with the Office of the Federal Register, issued guidelines with respect to business document retention. FIGURE 2-8 summarizes the recommendations that are applicable to personal documents.

Fig. 2-1A.

PERSONAL DATA SHEET
Spouse #1

Name _____
           (First)   (Middle)   (Last)

Residence Address _____
        (Street or P.O. Box)   (Apt.)

_____
      (City)   (State)   (Zip)

Social Security Number_____–_____–_____

Birthdate_____
       (M/D/Y)

Birthplace _____
     (City)   (County)   (State)   (Country)

Resident   of_____ **Since**_____
     (County)   (State)   (Month)   (Year)

Marital Status: ☐ **Single** ☐ **Married** ☐ **Divorced** ☐ **Widowed** ☐ **Separated**

Marriage_____
    (Date)   (City)   (County)   (State)

Spouse's   Name_____
      (First)   (Middle)   (Maiden)   (Last)

  Birthdate_____ **Birthplace** _____
          M/D/Y   (County)   (State)   (Country)

Father's Name_____
      (First)   (Middle)   (Last)

  Birthdate_____ **Birthplace** _____
          M/D/Y   (County) (State) (Country)

Mother's Name _____
      (First)   (Middle)   (Maiden)   (Last)

  Birthdate_____ **Birthplace** _____
         M/D/Y   (County) (State) (Country)

Occupation _____

  Employed by _____
  Since _____
        (Name) (City) (State)   (Month)   (Year)
  Type of Business_____

U.S. Veteran: ☐ **Yes** ☐ **No**
  Branch of Service_____
  Serial   Number_____
  Dates Served _____
             (From)   (To)

  Organization _____
  Rank _____
  Enlisted_____
         (Place)   (Date)
  Discharged _____
         (Place)   (Date)
  Discharge Certificate _____
         (Type)   (Where Kept)

Fig. 2-1B.

PERSONAL DATA SHEET
Spouse #2

Name _____
         (First)   (Middle)   (Last)

Residence Address _____
              (Street or P.O. Box)   (Apt.)

_____
              (City)   (State)   (Zip)

Social Security Number_____-_____-_____

Birthdate_____
              (M/D/Y)

Birthplace_____
              (City)   (County)   (State)   (Country)

Resident   of_____ **Since**_____
              (County)   (State)   (Month)   (Year)

Marital Status: ☐ **Single** ☐ **Married** ☐ **Divorced** ☐ **Widowed** ☐ **Separated**

Marriage_____
              (Date)   (City)   (County)   (State)

Spouse's   Name_____
              (First)   (Middle)   (Maiden)   (Last)

   Birthdate_____ **Birthplace** _____
              M/D/Y   (County)   (State)   (Country)

Father's Name_____
              (First)   (Middle)   (Last)

   Birthdate_____ **Birthplace** _____
              M/D/Y   (County)   (State) (Country)

Mother's Name _____
              (First)   (Middle)   (Maiden)   (Last)

   Birthdate_____ **Birthplace** _____
              M/D/Y   (County)   (State) (Country)

Occupation _____

   Employed by _____

   Since _____
              (Name)   (City)   (State)   (Month)   (Year)

   Type of Business_____

U.S. Veteran: ☐ **Yes** ☐ **No**

   Branch of Service_____

   Serial Number_____

   Dates Served _____
                          (From)   (To)

   Organization _____

   Rank _____

   Enlisted_____
                          (Place)   (Date)

   Discharged _____
                          (Place)   (Date)

   Discharge Certificate _____
                          (Type)   (Where Kept)

Fig. 2-2A (Page 1 of 2)

IMPORTANT DOCUMENTS
Spouse #1

Safe-Deposit Box:

Location _____

(Name of Institution)

_____

(Street Address)

_____

(City)   (State)

Location of Keys _____

_____

Executor:

Name _____

(First)   (Middle)   (Last)

Address _____

(Street Address)

_____

(City)   (State)   (Zip)

Phone (   ) _____

Location of Documents (write "SDB" if safe-deposit box):

Birth Certificate _____

Children's Birth Certificates _____

_____

Marriage Certificate _____

Deeds and Titles _____

_____

Mortgages and Notes _____

_____

Last Will and Testament _____

_____

Income Tax Records _____

_____

Fig. 2-2A (Page 2 of 2)

Annuities _____

_____

Certificates of Deposit_____

_____

Stock Certificates _____

_____

Insurance Policies_____

_____

Other Documents _____

_____

_____

_____

_____

_____

_____

_____

_____

_____

_____

_____

_____

_____

_____

_____

_____

_____

_____

_____

_____

_____

_____

Note: In most states, upon death, a decedent's safe-deposit box cannot be entered except in the presence of a tax agent or until an executor or administrator has been appointed.

Fig. 2-2B (Page 1 of 2)

IMPORTANT DOCUMENTS
Spouse #2

Safe-Deposit Box:

Location _____
(Name of Institution)

_____
(Street Address)

_____
(City)   (State)

Location of Keys _____

_____

Executor:

Name _____
(First)   (Middle)   (Last)

Address _____
(Street Address)

_____
(City)   (State)   (Zip)

Phone ( ) _____

Location of Documents (write "SDB" if safe-deposit box):

Birth Certificate _____

Children's Birth Certificates _____

_____

Marriage Certificate _____

Deeds and Titles _____

_____

Mortgages and Notes _____

_____

Last Will and Testament _____

_____

Income Tax Records _____

_____

Fig. 2-2B (Page 2 of 2)

Annuities _____

_____

Certificates of Deposit _____

_____

Stock Certificates _____

_____

Insurance Policies _____

_____

Other Documents _____

_____

_____

_____

_____

_____

_____

_____

_____

_____

_____

_____

_____

_____

_____

_____

_____

_____

_____

_____

_____

_____

Note: In most states, upon death, a decedent's safe-deposit box cannot be entered except in the presence of a tax agent or until an executor or administrator has been appointed.

Fig. 2-3A

LIFE INSURANCE POLICIES
Spouse #1

Company _____
 Policy Number_____
 Name of Insured_____
 Beneficiary _____
 Amount of Benefit $_____

Company _____
 Policy Number_____
 Name of Insured_____
 Beneficiary _____
 Amount of Benefit $_____

Company _____
 Policy Number_____
 Name of Insured_____
 Beneficiary _____
 Amount of Benefit $_____

Total Benefits $_____

The above policies are located in_____
_____
_____

Notes: 1. Annual review of beneficiaries will help prevent problems for survivors.
   2. Each insurer will require a certified copy of the death certificate.
   3. Duplicate this form and give a copy to someone outside your home. Others should be aware of your policies in the event of multiple deaths.

Fig. 2-3B

LIFE INSURANCE POLICIES
Spouse #2

Company _____

    Policy Number_____

    Name of Insured_____

    Beneficiary _____

    Amount of Benefit $_____

Company _____

    Policy Number_____

    Name of Insured_____

    Beneficiary _____

    Amount of Benefit $_____

Company _____

    Policy Number_____

    Name of Insured_____

    Beneficiary _____

    Amount of Benefit $_____

Total Benefits $_____

The above policies are located in_____

_____

_____

Notes: 1. Annual review of beneficiaries will help prevent problems for survivors.

    2. Each insurer will require a certified copy of the death certificate.

    3. Duplicate this form and give a copy to someone outside your home. Others should be aware of your policies in the event of multiple deaths.

Fig. 2-4A (Page 1 of 2)

BANK ACCOUNTS
Spouse #1 and/or Jointly Held

Checking:

  Institution_____

  Branch Address_____

  _____

  Account Number _____

  Institution_____

  Branch Address_____

  _____

  Account Number_____

Savings:

  Institution_____

  Branch Address_____

  _____

  Account Number _____

  Institution_____

  Branch Address_____

  _____

  Account Number _____

  Institution_____

  Branch Address_____

  _____

  Account Number _____

Fig. 2-4A (Page 2 of 2)

Certificates of Deposit (CDs):

Institution _____

Branch Address _____

_____

Account Number _____

Maturity Date _____

Institution _____

Branch Address _____

_____

Account Number _____

Maturity Date _____

Institution _____

Branch Address _____

_____

Account Number _____

Maturity Date _____

Fig. 2-4B (Page 1 of 2)

BANK ACCOUNTS
Spouse #2

Checking:

Institution_____

Branch Address_____

_____

Account Number _____

Institution_____

Branch Address_____

_____

Account Number _____

Savings:

Institution_____

Branch Address_____

_____

Account Number _____

Institution_____

Branch Address_____

_____

Account Number _____

Institution_____

Branch Address_____

_____

Account Number _____

Fig. 2-4B (Page 2 of 2)

Certificates of Deposit (CDs):

Institution _____

Branch Address _____

_____

Account Number _____

Maturity Date _____

Institution _____

Branch Address _____

_____

Account Number _____

Maturity Date _____

Institution _____

Branch Address _____

_____

Account Number _____

Maturity Date _____

Fig. 2-5A (Page 1 of 4)

INVESTMENTS, BUSINESS INTERESTS, REAL AND PERSONAL PROPERTY

Spouse #1 and/or Jointly Held

Trust Deeds, Notes, Accounts Receivable:

Debtor _____

Type of Debt _____

Amount $_____ **Due Date** _____

Debtor _____

Type of Debt _____

Amount $_____ **Due Date** _____

Debtor _____

Type of Debt _____

Amount $_____ **Due Date** _____

Debtor _____

Type of Debt _____

Amount $_____ **Due Date** _____

Mutual Funds:

Company _____

Number of Shares_____

Value $ _____ **as of** _____
                                                                    (Date)

Company _____

Number of Shares_____

Value $ _____ **as of** _____
                                                                    (Date)

Fig. 2-5A (Page 2 of 4)

Stocks:

Corporation _____

Number of Shares_____ Type_____

Value $ _____ as of _____
(Date)

Corporation _____

Number of Shares_____ Type_____

Value $ _____ as of _____
(Date)

Corporation _____

Number of Shares_____ Type_____

Value $ _____ as of _____
(Date)

Corporation _____

Number of Shares_____ Type_____

Value $ _____ as of _____
(Date)

Corporation _____

Number of Shares_____ Type_____

Value $ _____ as of _____
(Date)

Bonds:

Issuing Entity _____

Face Value $_____ Maturity Date_____

Value $ _____ as of _____
(Date)

Issuing Entity _____

Face Value $ _____ Maturity Date _____

Value $ _____ as of _____
(Date)

Individual Retirement Accounts (IRAs):

Institution_____

Type _____ Account Number _____

Balance $ _____ as of _____
(Date)

Fig. 2-5A (Page 3 of 4)

Institution_____

Type _____ **Account Number** _____

Balance $ _____ **as of** _____
                                                                    (Date)

Institution_____

Type _____ **Account Number** _____

Balance $ _____ **as of** _____
                                                                    (Date)

Retirement Plans (Pension, Profit-Sharing, Keogh, SEP, 401K, etc.):

Institution_____

Type _____ **Account Number** _____

Vested Amount $_____ **as of**_____
                                                                    (Date)

Institution_____

Type _____ **Account Number** _____

Vested Amount $_____ **as of**_____
                                                                    (Date)

Real Estate:

Residence: Address_____
                                                (Street Address)

_____
(City)   (County)   (State)   (Zip)

Appraised Value $_____ **as of**_____
                                                                    (Date)

First Mortgage Holder_____
                                                                    (Name)

_____
                                                (Address)

Balance $_____ **as of**_____
                                                                    (Date)

Second Mortgage Holder_____
                                                                    (Name)

_____
                                                (Address)

Balance $_____ **as of**_____
                                                                    (Date)

Other Property: Address_____
                                                (Street Address)

_____
(City)   (County)   (State)   (Zip)

Fig. 2-5A (Page 4 of 4)

Type of Property_____

Appraised Value $_____ **as of**_____
(Date)

Other Property: Address_____
(Street Address)

_____
(City)   (County)   (State)   (Zip)

Type of Property_____

Appraised Value $_____ **as of**_____
(Date)

Business Interests

Name of Business_____

Type: ☐ Sole Proprietorship ☐ General Partnership
☐ Limited Partnership ☐ Corporation

If Partnership, Names of Partners_____

_____

Name of Business_____

Type: ☐ Sole proprietorship ☐ General Partnership
☐ Limited Partnership ☐ Corporation

If Partnership, Names of Partners_____

_____

Personal Property:

Jewelry (>$1000 per piece)_____

_____

Furs (>$1000)_____

_____

Antiques or other exceptionally valuable furniture_____

_____

_____

Other (collections, artwork, boats, planes, recreational vehicles, mobile homes, burial plots)_____

_____

_____

Fig. 2-5B (Page 1 of 4)

INVESTMENTS, BUSINESS INTERESTS, REAL AND PERSONAL PROPERTY
Spouse #2

Trust Deeds, Notes, Accounts Receivable:

Debtor _____

Type of Debt _____

Amount $_____   **Due Date** _____

Debtor _____

Type of Debt _____

Amount $_____   **Due Date** _____

Debtor _____

Type of Debt _____

Amount $_____   **Due Date** _____

Debtor _____

Type of Debt _____

Amount $_____   **Due Date** _____

Mutual Funds:

Company _____

Number of Shares_____

Value $ _____   **as of** _____
                                                          (Date)

Company _____

Number of Shares_____

Value $ _____   **as of** _____

Fig. 2-5B (Page 2 of 4)

Stocks:

Corporation _____

Number of Shares_____   Type_____

Value $ _____   as of _____
                                                                     (Date)

Corporation _____

Number of Shares_____   Type_____

Value $ _____   as of _____
                                                                     (Date)

Corporation _____

Number of Shares_____   Type_____

Value $ _____   as of _____
                                                                     (Date)

Corporation _____

Number of Shares_____   Type_____

Value $ _____   as of _____
                                                                     (Date)

Corporation _____

Number of Shares_____   Type_____

Value $ _____   as of _____
                                                                     (Date)

Bonds:

Issuing Entity _____

Face Value $_____   Maturity Date_____

Value $ _____   as of _____
                                                                     (Date)

Issuing Entity _____

Face Value $ _____   Maturity Date _____

Value $ _____   as of _____
                                                                     (Date)

Individual Retirement Accounts (IRAs):

Institution_____

Type _____   Account Number _____

Balance $ _____   as of _____
                                                                     (Date)

Fig. 2-5B (Page 3 of 4)

Institution_____

Type _____   **Account Number** _____

Balance $ _____   **as of** _____
(Date)

Institution_____

Type _____   **Account Number** _____

Balance $ _____   **as of** _____
(Date)

Retirement Plans (Pension, Profit-Sharing, Keogh, SEP, 401K, etc.):

Institution_____

Type _____   **Account Number** _____

Vested Amount $_____   **as of**_____
(Date)

Institution_____

Type _____   **Account Number** _____

Vested Amount $_____   **as of**_____
(Date)

Real Estate:

Residence: Address_____
(Street Address)

_____
(City)   (County)   (State)   (Zip)

Appraised Value $_____   **as of**_____
(Date)

First Mortgage Holder_____
(Name)

_____
(Address)

Balance $_____   **as of**_____
(Date)

Second Mortgage Holder_____
(Name)

_____
(Address)

Balance $_____   **as of**_____
(Date)

Other Property: Address_____
(Street Address)

_____
(City)   (County)   (State)   (Zip)

Fig. 2-5B (Page 4 of 4)

Type of Property_____

Appraised Value $_____ as of_____
(Date)

Other Property: Address_____
(Street Address)

_____
(City)   (County)   (State)   (Zip)

Type of Property_____

Appraised Value $_____ as of_____
(Date)

Business Interests

Name of Business_____

Type: ☐ Sole Proprietorship ☐ General Partnership
☐ Limited Partnership ☐ Corporation

If Partnership, Names of Partners_____

_____

Name of Business_____

Type: ☐ Sole proprietorship ☐ General Partnership
☐ Limited Partnership ☐ Corporation

If Partnership, Names of Partners_____

_____

Personal Property:

Jewelry (>$1000 per piece)_____

_____

Furs (>$1000)_____

_____

Antiques or other exceptionally valuable furniture_____

_____

_____

Other (collections, artwork, boats, planes, recreational vehicles, mobile homes, burial plots)_____

_____

_____

Fig. 2-6 (Page 1 of 2)

FAMILY EMERGENCY CONTACTS

Relatives:

Relationship _____

Name _____

Address _____
(Street Address)

_____
(City)   (State)   (Zip)

Phone (   ) _____   **(   )** _____

Relationship _____

Name _____

Address _____
(Street Address)

_____
(City)   (State)   (Zip)

Phone (   ) _____   **(   )** _____

Relationship _____

Name _____

Address _____
(Street Address)

_____
(City)   (State)   (Zip)

Phone (   ) _____   **(   )** _____

Friends:

Name _____

Address _____
(Street Address)

_____
(City)   (State)   (Zip)

Phone (   ) _____   **(   )** _____

Fig. 2-6 (Page 2 of 2)

Name _____

Address _____
(Street Address)

_____
(City)   (State)   (Zip)

Phone (   ) _____   **(   )** _____

Funeral Director:

Name _____

Address _____
(Street Address)

_____
(City)   (State)   (Zip)

Phone (   ) _____   **(   )** _____

Attorney:

Name _____

Address _____
(Street Address)

_____
(City)   (State)   (Zip)

Phone (   ) _____   **(   )** _____

Accountant:

Name _____

Address _____
(Street Address)

_____
(City)   (State)   (Zip)

Phone (   ) _____   **(   )** _____

Doctor:

Name _____

Address _____
(Street Address)

_____
(City)   (State)   (Zip)

Phone (   ) _____   **(   )** _____

Fig. 2-7A (Page 1 of 2)

FUNERAL INSTRUCTIONS
Spouse #1

Place of Service_____
(Name)

_____
(Street Address)

_____   **Phone (   )**_____
(City)   (State)

Participating Organization (military or fraternal)_____

Open to the Public: ☐ Yes ☐ No

Casket: ☐ Metal ☐ Wood ☐ Fiberglass

Color (exterior) _____

Color and Material (interior)_____

Display: ☐ Open ☐ Closed

Flag: ☐ None   ☐ Fold, Place at Head of Casket   ☐ Drape Casket

Clothing: ☐ From Current Wardrobe ☐ New ☐ Other_____

Wedding Ring: ☐ Yes ☐ No

Stays on: ☐ Yes ☐ No, return to:_____

Other Jewelry_____

Stays on: ☐ Yes ☐ No, return to:_____

Music:

Organist: ☐ No ☐ Yes, selections_____

_____

Soloist: ☐ No ☐ Yes, selections_____

_____

Reading: ☐ No ☐ Yes, selections_____

_____

Cemetery:_____
(Name)

_____
(Street Address)

Fig. 2-7A (Page 2 of 2)

_____
(City)   (State)

Phone (   )_____

Location of Cemetery Deed_____

_____

Exchange Privileges: ☐ Yes   ☐ No

Cemetery Space to Be Used:

  ☐ Mausoleum   ☐ Lawn Crypt   ☐ Space

  Crypt/Space Number_____

Cemetery Space Preferred (if not pre-purchased):

  ☐ Mausoleum   ☐ Lawn Crypt   ☐ Space

Vault _____

Flower Container _____

Memorial: ☐ Bronze   ☐ Granite   ☐ Other

Inscription _____

_____

Emblem_____

Flowers_____
                               (Color or Type)

Special Instructions_____

_____

_____

_____

_____

_____

_____

_____

_____

_____

_____

_____

_____

_____

_____

Fig. 2-7B (Page 1 of 2)

FUNERAL INSTRUCTIONS
Spouse #2

Place of Service_____
(Name)

_____
(Street Address)

_____ **Phone (   )**_____
(City)   (State)

Participating Organization (military or fraternal)_____

Open to the Public: ☐ Yes ☐ No

Casket: ☐ Metal ☐ Wood ☐ Fiberglass

  Color (exterior) _____

  Color and Material (interior)_____

  Display: ☐ Open ☐ Closed

Flag: ☐ None   ☐ Fold, Place at Head of Casket   ☐ Drape Casket

Clothing: ☐ From Current Wardrobe ☐ New ☐ Other_____

Wedding Ring: ☐ Yes   ☐ No

  Stays on: ☐ Yes ☐ No, return to:_____

Other Jewelry_____

  Stays on: ☐ Yes ☐ No, return to:_____

Music:

  Organist: ☐ No ☐ Yes, selections_____

  _____

  Soloist: ☐ No ☐ Yes, selections_____

  _____

  Reading: ☐ No ☐ Yes, selections_____

  _____

Cemetery: _____
(Name)

_____
(Street Address)

Fig. 2-7B (Page 2 of 2)

_____
(City)   (State)

Phone (   )_____

Location of Cemetery Deed_____

_____

Exchange Privileges: ☐ Yes   ☐ No

Cemetery Space to Be Used:

☐ Mausoleum   ☐ Lawn Crypt   ☐ Space

Crypt/Space Number_____

Cemetery Space Preferred (if not pre-purchased):

☐ Mausoleum   ☐ Lawn Crypt   ☐ Space

Vault _____

Flower Container _____

Memorial: ☐ Bronze   ☐ Granite   ☐ Other

Inscription _____

_____

Emblem_____

Flowers_____
                              (Color or Type)

Special Instructions_____

_____

_____

_____

_____

_____

_____

_____

_____

_____

_____

_____

_____

Fig. 2-8

RETENTION OF RECORDS

Accident reports/claims (settled cases)	7 years
Bank reconciliations	2 years
Bank statements	3 years
Capital stock and bond records: ledgers transfer registers, stubs showing issues, record of interest coupons, options, etc.	Permanently
Checks (canceled—see exception below)	7 years
Checks (canceled for important payments, i.e. taxes, purchases of property, special contracts, etc. Checks should be filed with the papers pertaining to the underlying transaction)	Permanently
Contracts, mortgages, notes, and leases (expired)	7 years
Correspondence (general)	2 years
Correspondence (legal and important matters only)	Permanently
Deeds, mortgages, and bills of sale	Permanently
Depreciation schedules	Permanently
Duplicate deposit slips	2 years
Insurance policies (expired)	3 years
Insurance records, current accident reports, claims, policies, etc.	Permanently
Invoices (to customers, from vendors)	7 years
Notes receivable ledgers and schedules	7 years
Patents and related papers	Permanently
Property appraisals	Permanently
Property records, including costs, depreciation reserves, year-end trial balances, depreciation schedules, blueprints, and plans	Permanently
Retirement and pension records	Permanently
Tax returns, worksheets, and other documents relating to determination of income tax liability	7 years
Trademark registrations and copyrights	Permanently
Withholding tax statements	7 years

I've been rich, and I've been poor. Rich is better!—*Sophie Tucker*

3

Your Net Worth

Assets vs. Liabilities

THE FIRST AREA TO CONSIDER IS YOUR PERSONAL NET WORTH, that is, your assets less your liabilities. You can calculate this amount by preparing a *net worth statement*. A net worth statement simply consists of a listing of your assets and liabilities by major categories.

FIGURE 3-1 is a blank net worth worksheet for you to photocopy, but other formats will suffice. FIGURE 3-2 is a completed example of the same form. The family in this example has a net worth of $41,750. That is, their total assets exceed their total liabilities by $41,750. Since there is a positive net worth (assets exceed liabilities), the family is not in a critical financial situation. Their goal now is simply to accumulate wealth.

If the situation were reversed, and liabilities exceeded assets, there would be a crisis, and all aspects of the family's financial condition would need review to alleviate the crisis. Once the situation is under control, the goal becomes wealth accumulation.

If you are satisfied with your net worth, congratulations! You are well on your way. If you are not satisfied, read on. Increasing net worth is the goal of this book, and you now know your starting point.

Fig. 3-1 (Page 1 of 3)

Net Worth Statement

as of_____
(Date)

ASSETS

CASH:

10% Off the Top Fund $ _____

On Hand   _____

Checking Account   _____

Savings Account   _____

LOANS RECEIVABLE   _____

LIFE INSURANCE (cash surrender value)   _____

REAL ESTATE (current market value):

Home   _____

Other   _____

INVESTMENTS (current market value):

Stocks   _____

Bonds   _____

U.S. Savings Bonds   _____

Fig. 3-1 (Page 2 of 3)

Mutual Funds	_____
Other	_____
PERSONAL PROPERTY	
Automobiles	_____
Furniture	_____
Jewelry	_____
Furs	_____
Other	_____
RETIREMENT PLANS	
IRA	_____
Keogh	_____
Employer (vested amount)	_____
Other	_____
TOTAL ASSETS	$ _____

LIABILITIES

CURRENT BILLS:

Household/Utilities	$ _____
Taxes	_____
Medical	_____

Fig. 3-1 (Page 3 of 3)

Store Accounts/Credit Cards   _____

Other   _____

MORTGAGES:

Home   _____

Other   _____

LOANS PAYABLE:

Banks   _____

Autos   _____

Appliances   _____

Home Improvement   _____

Furniture   _____

Travel   _____

OTHER:

_____   _____

_____   _____

_____   _____

TOTAL LIABILITIES $ _____

TOTAL ASSETS $ _____

LESS: TOTAL LIABILITIES   (_____)

NET WORTH $ _____

Fig. 3-2 (Page 1 of 3)

Net Worth Statement

as of _February 1, 1989_
(Date)

ASSETS

CASH:

10% Off the Top Fund	$ 2,500
On Hand	250
Checking Account	500
Savings Account	1,000
LOANS RECEIVABLE	—o—
LIFE INSURANCE (cash surrender value)	—o—

REAL ESTATE (current market value):

Home	100,000
Other	—o—

INVESTMENTS (current market value):

Stocks	500
Bonds	—o—
U.S. Savings Bonds	1,000

Fig. 3-2 (Page 2 of 3)

Mutual Funds	500
Other	—0—

PERSONAL PROPERTY

Automobiles	10,000
Furniture	5,000
Jewelry	1,000
Furs	—0—
Other	—0—

RETIREMENT PLANS

IRA	4,000
Keogh	—0—
Employer (vested amount)	1,000
Other	—0—
TOTAL ASSETS	$ 127,250

LIABILITIES

CURRENT BILLS:

Household/Utilities	$ 500
Taxes	1,000
Medical	—0—

Fig. 3-2 (Page 3 of 3)

Store Accounts/Credit Cards	4,500
Other	—0—
MORTGAGES:	
Home	70,000
Other	—0—
LOANS PAYABLE:	
Banks	2,500
Autos	5,000
Appliances	—0—
Home Improvement	—0—
Furniture	2,000
Travel	—0—
OTHER:	
_____	—0—
_____	—0—
_____	—0—
TOTAL LIABILITIES	$ 85,500
TOTAL ASSETS	$ 127,250
LESS: TOTAL LIABILITIES	(85,500)
NET WORTH	$ 41,750

Jones: "How do you spend your income?"

Smith: "About 30% for shelter, 30% for clothing, 40% for food, and 20% for amusement."

Jones: "But, that adds up to 120%."

Smith: "That's right."

4

Budgeting

Controlling Your Income vs. Your Expenses

NOW THAT YOU KNOW WHAT YOU ARE WORTH, YOU NEED TO LOOK AT YOUR EXpected income and expenses. This exercise will give you a very clear picture of your current financial well-being.

If your income exceeds your expenses, great! If it doesn't, or you're not satisfied with the results, it's time to sharpen your pencil and begin to budget your expenses. You can set up a simple workable budget based on your own experience. The budget should be tailored to your income situation and geared to your individual goals.

Make money management a priority, and if you are getting married, make it a joint venture prior to your wedding day. Face your financial situation honestly and realistically. Stick to your budget until it works, but adjust the plan as circumstances dictate. Keep the following points in mind when beginning the budgeting process:

- You probably will try to spend more than you earn.

- Economy means *not* spending more than you earn.

- You will attain wealth only if you make it a part of what you spend.

- Your expenses are dictated by what you think you have available to spend, not by your needs.

- To accumulate wealth, you must add an "expense"—*10% Off the Top*.

When is a bargain not a bargain? When you don't need it. The best way to ruin a budget is to buy things you don't need. If you find it difficult to reduce expenses, try the following suggestions:

- Eliminate some expenses with the understanding that you are sacrificing only for a short time.
- Do things yourself instead of paying for services.
- Take advantage of free community educational and recreational services.

To get the most out of your money:

- Look for food specials and sales.
- Get information on a product before you purchase it.
- Comparison shop.
- Look for quality.
- Use credit wisely. Know what credit costs.
- Use a shopping list and adhere to it. Don't fall into the trap of impulse buying.

Have you heard the story of the two people discussing household budgeting? One says to the other, "Are you saving any money since you started your budget system?".

"Sure," the other says. "By the time we have it figured out every evening, it's too late to go anywhere."

Don't become totally absorbed in the budgeting process. An exact to-the-penny record is a waste of time.

The biggest obstacle to personal budgeting is normally the recordkeeping. You may not know where to start, or you just don't want to commit the time. So try the following for a year:

Use FIG. 4-1 to determine a target—a goal—for each month. This target should be realistic but impose enough pressure to reduce expenses.

To utilize this system effectively, determine the budgeted amount at the beginning of each month, and enter the actual expenses at the end of the month. During the month, you can review your budgeted expectations and use them as a guide for discretionary spending, e.g., eating out, cosmetics, etc.

One of the easiest ways to keep track of your expenses is to write checks for just about everything, but itemized credit card statements can serve the same purpose. And keep a record of any cash expenses as well. At the end of the month, sort out the checks by budget category, add up the checks for each category, and compare the totals to your budgeted amounts.

The results will influence and more accurately reflect the budget for the following month. They will also indicate areas that need to be reduced due to excesses that occurred in the previous months. Repeat this procedure each month.

At the end of the year prepare a year-to-date summary. The best budgeting results will be obtained from this summary, as there may be month-to-month variations due to annual insurance premiums, vacation expenses, etc. Also, variations will result if some checks fail to clear in a given month. The year-to-date summary will not suffer from these distortions.

The family in FIG. 4-2 had budgeted expenses of $3,908 for the month of January, but actually spent $4,734, exceeding the budget by $826. Based on the $4,570 they expected to earn for the month, they anticipated excess income of $662, while in actuality they spent $144 more than they earned. To cover that $144 deficit they had to use savings or incur additional debt.

Note that the *10% Off the Top* reflects 10% of the take-home income generated for the month (after withholding for taxes, social security, health insurance, etc). This 10% is considered an expense along with all of the other items. It helps you form a permanent habit of setting aside 10% routinely and automatically. Remember, you need to start somewhere. If 10% is too much to start with, try 5%, 1%, or even ½%. As your financial situation improves and/or the budgeting process eliminates or reduces other expenses, begin to increase that savings percentage toward the goal of *10% Off the Top*.

FIGURE 4-3 indicates the percentages that an average four-person household spends for various expense categories. The table is based on data from the U.S. Bureau of Labor Statistics. Use it to compare your spending patterns against the national norms. If you are above in some areas, you may want to reduce others. But, your budget is yours—and yours alone—and should be based on *your* personal needs and desires.

Fig. 4-1 (Page 1 of 4)

MONTHLY INCOME AND EXPENSE ANALYSIS

for _____ 19_____

	Budget –	*Actual* =	*Difference*
AVAILABLE INCOME:			
Salaries (after withholding)	$ _____	$ _____	$ _____
Interest & Dividends	_____	_____	_____
Other Sources	_____	_____	_____
Total Available Income	$ _____	$ _____	$ _____
EXPENSES:			
10% Off the Top	$ _____	$ _____	$ _____
Housing:			
Mortgage or Rent	_____	_____	_____
Homeowner's/Renter's Insurance	_____	_____	_____
Property Taxes	_____	_____	_____
Electric	_____	_____	_____
Gas	_____	_____	_____
Water	_____	_____	_____

Fig. 4-1 (Page 2 of 4)

Sanitation	_____	_____	_____
Telephone	_____	_____	_____
Cable TV	_____	_____	_____
Repairs/Appliances	_____	_____	_____
Miscellaneous	_____	_____	_____
Food	_____	_____	_____

Medical:

Doctors	_____	_____	_____
Dentist	_____	_____	_____
Drugs	_____	_____	_____
Miscellaneous	_____	_____	_____

Insurance Not Withheld:

Life	_____	_____	_____
Medical	_____	_____	_____
Disability	_____	_____	_____
Auto	_____	_____	_____
Miscellaneous	_____	_____	_____

Taxes Not Withheld:

Federal	_____	_____	_____

Fig. 4-1 (Page 3 of 4)

Social Security	_____	_____	_____
State	_____	_____	_____
Local	_____	_____	_____
Miscellaneous	_____	_____	_____
Transportation:			
Auto Payment	_____	_____	_____
Auto Repairs	_____	_____	_____
Gasoline/Oil	_____	_____	_____
License fees, taxes	_____	_____	_____
Bus, Taxi, and Other Fares	_____	_____	_____
Miscellaneous	_____	_____	_____
Clothing	_____	_____	_____
Education	_____	_____	_____
Entertainment:			
Restaurants	_____	_____	_____
Babysitting	_____	_____	_____
Vacation	_____	_____	_____
Movies/Plays	_____	_____	_____

Fig. 4-1 (Page 4 of 4)

Miscellaneous	_____	_____	_____
Miscellaneous:			
Cosmetics	_____	_____	_____
Toiletries	_____	_____	_____
Hair Styling	_____	_____	_____
Laundry	_____	_____	_____
Allowances	_____	_____	_____
Lunch Money	_____	_____	_____
Subscriptions	_____	_____	_____
Gifts	_____	_____	_____
Contributions	_____	_____	_____
Other	_____	_____	_____
Total Expenses	$ _____	$ _____	$ _____

Excess of Income over Expenses $ _____ $ _____

Fig. 4-2 (Page 1 of 4)

MONTHLY INCOME AND EXPENSE ANALYSIS
for _February_ 19_89_

	Budget –	Actual =	Difference
AVAILABLE INCOME:			
Salaries (after withholding)	$ 4,320	$ 4,320	$ –0–
Interest & Dividends	250	270	(20)
Other Sources	–0–	–0–	–0–
Total Available Income	$ 4,570	$ 4,590	$ (20)
EXPENSES:			
10% Off the Top	$ 457	$ 459	$ (2)
Housing:			
Mortgage or Rent	450	450	–0–
Homeowner's/Renter's Insurance	55	55	–0–
Property Taxes	110	110	–0–
Electric	90	72	18
Gas	45	41	4
Water	30	42	(12)

Fig. 4-2 (Page 2 of 4)

Sanitation	15	19	(4)
Telephone	45	64	(19)
Cable TV	22	22	-0-
Repairs/Appliances	50	233	(183)
Miscellaneous	50	-0-	50
Food	200	187	13
Medical:			
Doctors	-0-	35	(35)
Dentist	-0-	-0-	-0-
Drugs	-0-	5	(5)
Miscellaneous	-0-	-0-	-0-
Insurance Not Withheld:			
Life	94	94	-0-
Medical	43	43	-0-
Disability	27	27	-0-
Auto	485	485	-0-
Miscellaneous	-0-	-0-	-0-
Taxes Not Withheld:			
Federal	70	76	(6)

Fig. 4-2 (Page 3 of 4)

Social Security	-0-	-0-	-0-
State	5	6	(1)
Local	2	3	(1)
Miscellaneous	-0-	-0-	-0-
Transportation:			
Auto Payment	171	171	-0-
Auto Repairs	25	683	(658)
Gasoline/Oil	40	51	(11)
License fees, taxes	50	50	-0-
Bus, Taxi, and Other Fares	-0-	-0-	-0-
Miscellaneous	-0-	-0-	-0-
Clothing	140	83	57
Education	750	750	-0-
Entertainment:			
Restaurants	50	62	(12)
Babysitting	55	41	14
Vacation	-0-	-0-	-0-
Movies/Plays	15	8	7

Fig. 4-2 (Page 4 of 4)

Miscellaneous	50	66	(16)
Miscellaneous:			
Cosmetics	10	25	(15)
Toiletries	10	12	(2)
Hair Styling	30	28	2
Laundry	35	28	7
Allowances	20	20	-0-
Lunch Money	80	99	(19)
Subscriptions	12	12	-0-
Gifts	-0-	-0-	-0-
Contributions	-0-	5	(5)
Other	20	12	8
Total Expenses	$ 3,908	$ 4,734	$ (826)

Excess of Income over Expenses $ 662 $ (144)

Fig. 4-3

AVERAGE EXPENSE PERCENTAGES

Four-Person Family

Expense Category	Standard of Living		
	Lower	Middle	Upper
Food	30%	23%	19%
Housing	18	22	23
Transportation	9	9	8
Clothing	6	5	5
Personal Care	2	2	2
Medical Care	10	6	4
Other Miscellaneous	4	5	5
	79	72	66
Social Security Disability	4	7	5
Personal Income Taxes	10	17	25
Other Miscellaneous Taxes	4	4	4
	100%	100%	100%

Columns may not total to 100% due to rounding.

Overheard on the beach:

"Mommy, may I go in for a swim?"
"Certainly not, my dear, it's far too deep."
"But Daddy is swimming."
"I know, dear, but he's insured."

5

Insurance

Protection from the Unexpected

YOU NEED TO PROTECT YOURSELF FROM THE UNEXPECTED, WHETHER IT BE OF A financial or a personal nature. You can partially accomplish this by having sufficient emergency funds in the form of a cash reserve and by maintaining a well-thought-out investment program, but disability and life insurance are also important factors. Insurance generally cannot be considered an investment and does not increase your wealth, but it is one method of protecting your accumulated wealth.

The first thing you need to consider is which risks you can cover yourself (self-insurance) and which you will need protection against. Insurance companies exist for the latter purpose. There is a cost associated with each strategy. Certain areas lend themselves to self-insurance, depending on your level of cash reserves and "liquid" investments (ones that can be turned into cash easily and quickly). In other cases, no matter what amount of your cash reserves and liquid investments you have, it is less expensive to buy insurance.

CASH RESERVES

A cash reserve is the first step in planning for emergencies. In addition to currency on hand, funds deposited in checking and savings accounts are usually quickly available. Other liquid assets are short-term certificates of deposit (CDs) and money-market funds, which can be converted to cash within a few days.

A practical rule of thumb: The equivalent of one month's income, plus three months of debt payments, should be kept in very liquid reserves. For example, if your debts amount to a monthly payment of $200, you should have $600, plus one month's salary, available in cash reserve.

Don't count your *10% Off the Top* fund in the above calculation. This fund is for investment growth and wealth accumulation. This is not a fund to cover emergencies unless *absolutely necessary*.

RISK AND INSURANCE

Insurance is simply a plan for dealing with the risk of economic loss resulting from a future unexpected event. You purchase fire insurance because of the risk that your property may be destroyed by fire. You purchase life insurance because of the risk of the economic loss resulting from death. In each case the insurer protects you by guaranteeing to pay a stated or ascertainable amount of money to a specified person if the loss occurs.

By purchasing insurance you transfer to the insurer the risk of loss. You exchange a risk of a large potential loss for a certain but much smaller loss: the cost of the insurance premium.

LIFE INSURANCE

In at least one respect, a life insurance policy is the worst "investment" you will ever make! You are betting that you will die, while the insurer is betting that you will live. Life insurance, however, is one of the necessary "evils" of your financial well-being. In addition, insurance companies have developed many policies which offer some investment opportunity.

Your sudden death would most likely have a dramatic effect on the economics of your surviving family. The purpose of life insurance is to avoid this major disruption and to maintain the financial stability of your survivors. The amount of life insurance required to cover the income needs of your survivors depends on many factors. Probably the most important question is: How much additional annual income will be needed? This is determined by comparing any sources of income that will continue after your death (e.g., spouse's continuing income, interest income, etc.) to the amount of continuing expenses. Other considerations are the number of years the additional annual income will be required, the earning power of the remaining assets, and the effect of inflation on purchasing power. For peace of mind, you should try to have any debt, including the mortgage, paid off with the insurance proceeds.

FIGURE 5-1 should be used as a guide in determining the life insurance needs of you and your spouse. To cover contingencies and possible errors in the estimates, you may wish to have a greater amount of life insurance than the calculation indicates.

FIGURE 5-2 is an example of how the above table should be used to calculate your insurance needs. Assume that the surviving spouse (Spouse #2) has an annual salary of $20,000, including bonuses, etc.; that $5,000 of interest and dividends will be received on an annual basis from savings and investments; that no social security will be paid to the survivor; that the annual cost of maintaining the house and car and all of the other costs of living will amount to $30,000; that there are no children to support; that the balance on the mortgage is $85,000 and the other loans total $5,000; and that the survivor will probably need to be protected from the loss of income for 10 years. The number of years can either be based on life expectancy or the date when other income, such as retirement funds or social security, will begin.

Based on the above, $140,000 of life insurance would be required. If the mortgage payoff of $85,000 was not desired, the insurance needed would be reduced accordingly. However, the annual living expenses would need to be increased to cover the 12 monthly mortgage payments which would continue.

Types of Life Insurance

Now that you know how much life insurance to purchase, you must choose from among the various types of life insurance available.

Term Insurance. Term insurance is temporary insurance, that is, it runs for a period of time—1, 5, 10 years, etc. You pay a stated premium during the term, and, assuming you don't die, the policy expires at the end of the term, and the coverage ends. Most term policies do allow you to renew up to age 65 or 70, but on each renewal there is an often substantial increase in premiums. Many policies offer a conversion to permanent coverage, and some do not require a physical exam.

Initially, term insurance is the least expensive type of insurance. As time goes on, it can become more expensive than other forms of coverage.

Ordinary Life. Ordinary life is a form of *whole life insurance*. It is permanent insurance that will pay off any time the insured dies, rather than within a specific time period. Under this arrangement you pay a fixed premium during your lifetime, and you have continuous coverage. As you pay premiums, you build up a cash value within the policy. In many cases, after three to five years, the cash value buildup each year will exceed your annual premium. Note, also, that as this cash value builds, you continue to be protected by the life insurance. This cash value is available for borrowing—and generally at very favorable interest rates. In addition, if you decide that you no longer want the insurance protection you can withdraw the cash value of the policy.

From a tax point of view, the cash buildup is not subject to taxation. But if you terminate the policy and take the cash value, you pay tax on the amount withdrawn which exceeds the premiums previously paid in.

Variable Life. Variable life is very similar to ordinary life or whole life in that you pay a fixed premium, accumulate a cash value, and have a death benefit. However, variable life offers greater investment opportunity with respect to the cash-value buildup—you can have that cash value invested in stocks, bonds, money market funds, or other types of investment vehicles. You can also change the investment vehicle at any time, if you so desire. Obviously, the cash value is affected by the results of the investment you have chosen and thus can fluctuate, but you are fully covered by the life insurance at all times, regardless of the investment gains or losses.

Universal Life. Universal life is basically a combination of term insurance and an investment program. There are no fixed premiums with this type of insurance. Instead, you make an initial premium payment. The continued growth of that initial payment is then reduced annually to cover your insurance cost. As long as there are sufficient assets in your account you are not required to make any additional payments, and your insurance protection continues. The cash value of your account can be invested in stocks, bonds, etc., and can be changed as you desire.

Limited-Payment Life. Limited-payment life is very similar to ordinary life except that you pay premiums for a specified period, such as 10 or 20 years, or until you reach a certain age. After that, the policy is completely paid for, and the life insurance coverage remains in effect.

Paid-Up Life. Paid-up life insurance is very similar to limited-payment life except that you pay the entire premium in one payment.

Single-Premium Life. The single-premium life insurance policy is similar to paid-up life but is also an investment vehicle. Your lump-sum premium buys a greater amount of life insurance coverage than you would normally receive in a paid-up life policy. You then are given two investment choices. You may invest conservatively, with earnings that will vary as interest rates move up or down (the insurer will guarantee some minimal interest rate, for example, 4%), or you can invest in stocks, bonds, etc., similar to variable and universal-life programs.

Single-premium life offers attractive borrowing features with minimal tax consequences. The death benefit may vary with this type of policy depending on the earnings from your investment choice, so this type of policy should be considered as an investment with the additional benefit of insurance coverage.

Which Insurance to Choose

The easiest and least expensive life insurance, at least initially, is term insurance. For most people, this type is the major portion of their insurance program. However, other policies allow for additional investment earnings and growth while providing the insurance protection needed.

Give careful thought to this purchase. Ask questions and compare insurance companies and rates. In some circumstances, you might even decide to purchase a combination of term insurance and some type of whole-life policy to meet your needs.

DISABILITY INSURANCE

If you suddenly became disabled, you and your family would probably suffer a major financial setback. And there is probably more of a chance of your becoming disabled than of dying prematurely. Disability insurance is an excellent way of protecting yourself against this possibility.

To determine the amount of disability coverage you need, you must compare the income that will continue (spouse's salary, interest, dividends, etc.) to your monthly living expenses. Plus, you will need to cover the payment of estimated taxes, debts, and your children's educational expenses.

Although some of your monthly living expenses will probably decrease in the event of your disability, others, such as medical, will probably increase. Therefore, the estimate of your *current* living expenses will suffice as a guide. You can do a more precise analysis if you wish.

FIGURE 5-3 will help you determine the disability coverage you need. FIGURE 5-4, an example of how to make the calculation, assumes that there will not be any continuing salary for Spouse #1 (the disabled person), but that Spouse #2 will continue to earn $1,000 monthly; that interest and dividends will generate $500 monthly; that monthly household living expenses are $3,000; and that monthly taxes will be $500. Based on this, Spouse #1 should purchase a disability policy that will generate $2,000 per month in payments.

Because social security coverage is not included in this analysis, this estimate is conservative. The rules for the payment of disability benefits under the social security system are very narrow and strict, so these benefits were purposely left out. Even if you qualify, there is a long waiting period (generally 9 to 12 months) which tends to discourage any reliance on this source of income.

Insurance companies set limits on the maximum amount of monthly disability benefits. This limit is primarily based on your current monthly earned income, but you might be able to buy additional amounts with a limited coverage period (e.g., 12 months).

Eligibility for payments depends on what the policy defines as a disability. Some policies will cover a disability occurring in any occupation. Others specify an occupation and may not pay you any benefits if you can work in another occupation. If you were a surgeon and could no longer perform operations, you would want to be covered for that. You would not want the fact that you could also repair cars to preclude you from receiving monthly benefits.

Some policies will only pay benefits if you are totally disabled. Others cover partial disability; if you can return to your job but only earn a portion of your present income, they will pay all or part of the lost income. This could be a very important consideration where you are the sole support of your family.

You also need to consider the length of time that the policy will pay monthly benefits. The shorter the coverage period, the less expensive the policy. The most common policies pay for two years, five years, or to age 65. Normally, the most financially burdensome period is the first two years of disability.

And there are many other features to consider as well. Review the various options and possibilities with your insurance agent:

- Is the policy cancellable or non-cancellable by the insurer?

- What is the elimination period? (When does the policy start to pay benefits?)

- What is the qualification period? (When will partial disability coverage begin?)

- Is there a social security supplement? (Would the policy pay if you don't meet social security definitions?)

- Are there cost-of-living adjustments?

- Can you purchase additional coverage as your earned income increases?

If you have group coverage, review the policy features. Typically, these policies are very limited and contain few of the features discussed. Still, they are very inexpensive, so you may wish to purchase the coverage. But they generally should not be relied upon for your only disability coverage. The group policy is merely a supplement to the primary disability policy purchased individually.

Fig. 5-1

LIFE INSURANCE NEEDS

	Spouse #1	Spouse #2
Estimated Annual Living Expenses of Survivor	\$_____	\$_____
Less: Survivor's Annual Income Remaining		
Annual Wages, Bonuses, etc.	(____)	(____)
Annual Interest, Dividends, etc.	(____)	(____)
Annual Social Security Income	(____)	(____)
Other Annual Income	(____)	(____)
Excess Annual Living Expenses to be Covered by Insurance	\$____	\$____
Survivor's Life Expectancy (years remaining)[a]	X____	X____
Insurance Needed to Cover Living Expenses	\$____	\$____
Estimated Taxes	____	____
Debts to be Retired at Death	____	____
Children's Educational Needs	____	____
Additional Needs to be Covered	____	____
Less: Savings Survivor Wishes to Use	(____)	(____)
TOTAL LIFE INSURANCE NEEDED	\$____	\$____

[a]For the purposes of this calculation, enter the number of years remaining until age 80 or 85, or consult a life insurance agent.

Fig. 5-2

LIFE INSURANCE NEEDS

	Spouse #1	Spouse #2
Estimated Annual Living Expenses of Survivor	$ _____	$ 30,000
Less: Survivor's Annual Income Remaining		
Annual Wages, Bonuses, etc.	(_____)	(20,000)
Annual Interest, Dividends, etc.	(_____)	(5,000)
Annual Social Security Income	(_____)	(-0-)
Other Annual Income	(_____)	(-0-)
Excess Annual Living Expenses to be Covered by Insurance	$ _____	$ 5,000
Survivor's Life Expectancy (years remaining)[a]	X _____	X 10
Insurance Needed to Cover Living Expenses	$ _____	$ 50,000
Estimated Taxes	_____	-0-
Debts to be Retired at Death[b]	_____	90,000
Children's Educational Needs	_____	-0-
Additional Needs to be Covered	_____	-0-
Less: Savings Survivor Wishes to Use	(_____)	(-0-)
TOTAL LIFE INSURANCE NEEDED	$ _____	$ 140,000

[a]For the purposes of this calculation, enter the number of years remaining until age 80 or 85, or consult a life insurance agent.
[b]Upon the death of the first spouse to die, Spouse #1, there is an $85,000 balance due on the mortgage, a $3,000 balance due on an auto loan and $2,000 in credit card balances.

Fig. 5-3

DISABILITY INSURANCE NEEDS

	Spouse #1	Spouse #2
Monthly Earnings Continuing if Disabled	$_____	$_____
Other Continuing Monthly Income (i.e., inheritance, dividends, etc.)	_____	_____
Total Monthly Income	$_____	$_____
Less Monthly Living Expenses	(_____)	(_____)
Less Reserve for Income Taxes	(_____)	(_____)
MONTHLY DISABILITY INCOME NEEDED	$_____	$_____

Fig. 5-4.

DISABILITY INSURANCE NEEDS

	Spouse #1	Spouse #2
Monthly Earnings Continuing if Disabled	$ -0-	$ 1,000
Other Continuing Monthly Income (i.e., inheritance, dividends, etc.)	-0-	500
Total Monthly Income	$ -0-	$ 1,500
Less Monthly Living Expenses	(—)	(3,000)
Less Reserve for Income Taxes	(—)	(500)
MONTHLY DISABILITY INCOME NEEDED	$ —	$ 2,000

6

Providing for Your Children's Education

Preparing for the High Cost of Learning

THE COST OF EDUCATION HAS RISEN TO THE POINT WHERE IT IS LIKELY TO REP-
resent a large portion of your annual income. Aside from the purchase of a home
and planning for retirement, the financing of your children's education is possi-
bly your major financial responsibility. (For the most part we are concerned here
with college costs, but in some cases primary or secondary educational costs
may also require funding.) Planning can make the difference as to whether—and
where—your child will attend college.

To adequately plan for your children's educational needs, you must first iden-
tify your goals. You need to consider the type of college you wish to have your
child attend. The difference in cost between a private versus public university
can be significant. In addition, tuition costs vary greatly among the private schools,
with the Ivy League being the most expensive. Are you willing to sacrifice so
that your child can attend a private college? Or will public institutions be acceptable? Is there an overall maximum dollar amount that you will make available
to your child for college? Some parents I know gave their child $20,000 toward
college with all additional costs to be covered by the child.

Tuition costs have grown dramatically over the last several years. The average
private school has seen its tuition increase more than 10 percent a year since
1980. The U.S. Department of Education estimates that by the year 2007 the
total cost of a four-year college program will exceed $60,000 for a public univer-
sity and $200,000 for a private university.

FINANCING

A college education may be financed from your current income and assets. This, however, may place a great strain on your family.

Scholarships, grants, and loans can no longer be relied on to finance a college education due to significant federal and state cutbacks in recent years. And colleges consider the parents' and the child's income and savings in determining the amount of aid available, so based on the formulas used currently, fewer and fewer families are eligible for this aid.

The government has even reduced some of the tax advantages that were available. The interest expense deduction on unsecured college loans (not collateralized by your residence) is being phased out. This expense will be completely nondeductible by 1991.

Prior to the Tax Reform Act of 1986, education was often funded by shifting parental income to the children, who paid little or no taxes. The resultant tax savings permitted greater accumulation of funds for education. Under the new rules, however, a child under age 14 who receives property transferred directly or indirectly to him or her will pay tax at the parents' higher rate on any income generated in excess of $1,000. This provision is known as the "Kiddie Tax."

Financing Options

Transfer of Assets to Minors. Series EE bonds and similar types of investments can be given to minors. The tax on the interest from EE bonds can be deferred until the bonds are redeemed, avoiding the "Kiddie Tax." The eventual tax on the interest earned will most likely be at a low rate, because the child will likely be in college and not be in a high bracket.

Uniform Gifts to Minors Act. Certain types of assets, such as bank accounts, securities, and life insurance policies, may be transferred to minors under the Uniform Gifts to Minors Act. Not all states have adopted this Act, but in those states that have, all types of property may be transferred. These transfers are simple, but you must use caution. The parents cannot be custodians of the transferred property, or else the property will be included in the parents' estate. (An estate of $600,000 or less in total assets will not be subject to estate tax.) Another pitfall is the "Kiddie Tax," if the child is under 14.

Trusts. With the adoption of the 1986 Tax Reform Act, many of the benefits of trusts were diminished or eliminated. But at least two types of trusts continue to have merit. One such trust, under Section 2503(c) of the Internal Revenue Code, is a special trust for minors. The income generated within this trust can avoid the "Kiddie Tax." A second type, known as a "Crumey Trust," allows for the withdrawal of funds by the beneficiary. However, growth-type investments should be used to fund such a trust, because the "Kiddie Tax" will apply to the income generated. The trust area is extremely complicated and beyond the scope of this book. Obtain professional guidance.

Prepaying Tuition. A new concept has arisen in the last several years: the prepayment of college tuition while a child is still young. For most institutions this in no way guarantees that the child will be admitted, but refund and transferability provisions exist in the event admission is denied. Currently there are no tax ramifications to such a plan.

Insurance. Insurance policies with variable interest rates, on the life of a parent, can be useful for funding education. Some universal-life policies with withdrawal features can be useful as well, if the withdrawal is not considered merely a loan. Or a policy can be taken out on the life of a young child for his or her future education. A more complete discussion of life insurance policies is included in Chapter 5.

FINANCIAL AID

Obtaining financial aid has become increasingly difficult. Yet, several types of assistance programs exist. Applications and further information are available from college financial aid offices and many high school guidance counselors.

Guaranteed Student Loans. Guaranteed student loans (GSLs) are loans that are available from participating banks. These loans are subsidized by the federal government, so the interest rate charged is lower than normal bank loan rates. The maximum award is $2,500 per academic year. Generally, loans made directly to the student do not require repayment to begin until six months after the student leaves or graduates from school. The interest rate is 8%; however, if the parent takes out the loan, the interest rate is usually higher, and the repayment begins 60 days after the loan is funded. The repayment period is usually five to ten years. Applications for GSLs are available at participating banks, savings and loans, and credit unions.

Supplemental Education Opportunity Grants (SEOGs). The federal government provides funds to colleges to be used for students with financial need. The program does not set the financial need guidelines but leaves it up to the college to make the determination. Awards range from $200 to $2000 per academic year and can be renewed, pending continued evidence of financial need, satisfactory academic progress, and adequate funding levels.

The Pell Grant. Based on a student's need, the Pell Grant provides up to 60% of college expenses, not to exceed a maximum currently established at

$2,100. Congress determines an annual appropriation for this grant fund. Thus, the maximum grant per student is subject to change.

Parent Loans for Undergraduate Students (PLUS). This is a loan program similar to the GSL program. The maximum your child can receive is $3,000. Repayment begins 60 days after the loan is made, and an annual interest rate of 12% is charged. Students (including graduate students) may be directly eligible for these loans as well.

National Direct Student Loans. These loans, made directly to the student, are also subsidized by the federal government, but the college determines eligibility and administers the program. The maximum your child can borrow is $6,000 for undergraduate study. Repayment of the loan begins six months after the student graduates or leaves school, but can be postponed for an additional three-year period if the student is enrolled in graduate school or is in government service, such as the military or the Peace Corps.

College Work-Study Programs. The federal government subsidizes student employment within the various college departments. Generally, part-time jobs (average of 10 hours per week) are provided during the school year, and full-time jobs are provided during vacation periods. The colleges determine how much a student can earn in any one year.

State Financial Aid. Many states offer financial aid for state residents attending state schools. Some states provide some assistance to nonresidents as well.

Other Sources of Financial Aid. Most colleges have their own financial aid programs, scholarships, loans, and jobs. Some offer tuition payment plans, discounts for prepayment of the entire tuition upon initial enrollment, or reduced or no interest charges for a period of time.

Finally, check your library or bookstore for books that list various businesses, civic groups, and other organizations which provide financial aid. This type of aid is often based on merit or need, or is limited to members of specific groups, children of workers, or students who major in specific areas. There are a growing number of firms which, for a fee, will help you find this kind of financial aid.

DETERMINING YOUR "COLLEGE FUND"

Once you determine the anticipated cost of college, you will have a goal to strive for, even though in many cases you will never accumulate the entire required fund. The fund is often supplemented by the cash flow within the household at the time the children go off to college. To reduce the financial disruption this can cause, the greater the college fund, the better.

Complete FIG. 6-1 for each child. FIGURE 6-2 is an example of how to complete the form. The example shows that, in nine years, the Doe family will need $91,200 to put John through college. This is only an estimate, but it gives an idea as to what college costs will be when the time comes.

After you determine the amount you'll need, begin to plan accordingly. Start a savings plan, and as your child's college education draws near, explore the various financial aid programs. With proper advance planning, you can significantly reduce the enormous burden of putting a child through college and give your child the opportunity to attend the best possible school.

Fig. 6-1

College Fund Needed

Child's Name _____

Child's Age _____

A. Number of years remaining before college   _____

B. Anticipated number of years in college   _____

C. Estimated inflation rate for college costs   _____%

D. Estimated cost of one year of college currently $ _____

Estimated Future College Costs = B × D × [1 + (C × A)]

= ___× $_____ × [1 + (__% ×__)]

= $ _____

Fig. 6-2

College Fund Needed

Child's Name _John Doe_

Child's Age ___10___

A. Number of years remaining before college   _9_

B. Anticipated number of years in college   _4_

C. Estimated inflation rate for college costs   _10_%

D. Estimated cost of one year of college currently $_12,000_

Estimated Future College Costs = B × D × [1 + (C × A)]

$$= \underline{4} \times \$\underline{12,000} \times [\, 1 + (\underline{10}\% \times \underline{9})\,]$$

$$= \$\ \underline{91,200}$$

You can never plan the future by the past.—*Edmund Burke*

7

Retirement Planning

Opportunity and Challenge

RETIREMENT REQUIRES CAREFUL PLANNING, YET MOST PEOPLE DON'T PREPARE for it. Retirement goals and needs will more likely be met if financial planning begins early. Even in your 20s or 30s, when most of your financial assets are committed to housing, insurance, and education, you can start modest investment programs (*10% Off the Top*) and make annual contributions to pension plans or IRAs.

When you reach the magic age of 40, give retirement planning your full attention. At that point, if you had children in your early 20s, your family obligations may be on their way down, your children's education may be nearing completion, mortgage payments may represent a smaller portion of your income, and your earnings may be near their highest level.

For most people, a plan that begins at least 15 years in advance will enable them to set aside enough money for an enjoyable retirement. To plan for your retirement you need to analyze whether your present net worth could produce a sufficient amount of income to handle your living expenses after retirement. A rule of thumb is that retirement income needs are about 60-70% of pre-retirement income. You can obtain a more accurate estimate by completing FIG. 7-1. Many assumptions and estimates are required.

Don't be discouraged. Estimate as best you can. The results will at least give you a good indication of your financial progress towards your retirement.

In FIG. 7-2, an estimated retirement income and expense schedule completed for an individual at age 40, estimated expenses exceed estimated income by $11,700. The goal, however, is to create an excess of income over expenses to cover any contingencies or incorrect estimates. The 40-year-old subject of this example has approximately 25 years to work toward this goal.

PLANNING AND TAXES

Many types of retirement plans are given favorable tax treatment. Whether a plan is established by you or your employer, your participation allows you the following tax benefits:

- The amount contributed to the plan is, within limits, tax-deferred. In the case of employer plans, the amount contributed by the employer is excluded from your taxable wages. In those cases where an employer plan allows for employee contributions, those contributions will be deductible against your taxable income. In each case, the tax is deferred until you withdraw the funds. It is not avoided forever.

- The earnings of your retirement plan are taxed when they are withdrawn, not when earned.

- There is a strong possibility that, when you withdraw the funds, your tax rate will be lower than when the contributions were made. The reason for this is that your taxable income will most likely be lower after you retire, and for certain distributions, special favorable tax rates are available.

Keep in mind that the purpose of these plans is to provide you with funds for your retirement. Tax advantages serve as an incentive for you to fund these plans. You will face penalties if you withdraw the funds before you retire or reach a certain age. So consider these ramifications before participating in such a retirement program. If you know you will be withdrawing the funds but only want the tax advantages, these types of arrangements are currently not a wise investment.

TYPES OF PLANS

Individual Retirement Accounts (IRAs). Individual retirement accounts are discussed in detail in Chapter 10.

Keogh Plans. If you have net earnings from self-employment, you may be eligible to open and contribute to a special retirement plan for self-employed individuals, called a *Keogh plan*. You do not have to pursue your business full-time to be considered self-employed. Thus, if you work for a salary and, in addition, conduct a business from your home, the net earnings from that business are considered self-employment income.

You can contribute the lesser of 20% of your net self-employment income, or $30,000, to a Keogh plan. If you have employees, contributions may have to be made on their behalf as well.

The Keogh plan must be opened prior to the end of the tax year to be eligible. However, the entire contribution need not be made prior to year end; you have until April 15. So you might want to open a Keogh plan at a bank or brokerage firm by depositing a small amount (for example, $100) prior to year end and complete your contribution by April 15.

Employer-Sponsored Plans. In addition to creating your own plan, you may have the right to participate in a retirement plan established by your employer. The rules regarding employer-sponsored plans are very complicated.

You should know how your plan operates and be aware of the limitations on the amount of contributions that can be made. You also should be aware of whether or not you are entitled to make your own contribution to the plan and the limitations thereon, whether you can borrow funds from the plan, and when you can begin withdrawing funds. Your employer is required by law to provide you with a summary of the plan which must contain all of the above information.

Employer Pension Plans. A pension plan at work, if approved and qualified by the IRS, may allow for employee contributions. In some cases, only the earnings of the plan—not the contributions—are tax-deferred. Review your particular plan for this possibility.

401(K) Plans. Under a 401(K) plan you may elect to have your employer withhold contributions so that they will not be included in your taxable income for the year. The employer simply reduces your take-home salary by the amount of the contribution, and no tax is withheld on that amount. This arrangement is often known as a *salary reduction agreement*. Many employers make matching contributions that are based on a percentage of the amount you contribute.

Your personal contribution to a 401(K) plan is limited to a maximum of $7,000 annually. In the future, this limit will increase, based upon the inflation rate. In many cases, one year's employment may be required before you are eligible to participate in such a plan.

Corporate Savings Plan. Many corporate savings plans qualify for favored tax treatment and therefore are a valuable tool in retirement planning. The corporation, as well as the employee, contributes to the plan. Such plans generally operate in the following manner: You put a certain amount into the plan, up to a maximum of 10% of your salary. The corporation then matches your contribution at a fixed percentage (typically 50–100%), and all of the earnings within the plan are tax-deferred.

The vesting time of these plans varies. If you withdraw before you are vested, you forfeit the non-vested portion of the funds. You do not, however, forfeit the amount you contributed or the earnings thereon.

Simplified Employee Pension (SEP) Plans. Under a Simplified Employee Pension Plan, your employer can annually contribute up to $30,000, or 15% of your compensation, whichever is less. This plan must be nondiscriminatory and available to all employees. The contribution is made to each employee's own IRA account. In fact, if your employer contributes less than the IRA limit of $2,000, you may be able to contribute and deduct the difference, subject to the IRA rules on allowable contributions (see Chapter 10).

You can participate in other qualified retirement plans and also be included in a SEP.

TAX-ADVANTAGEOUS INVESTMENTS

In addition to the various plans described above, you should consider other tax-advantageous investments in building toward retirement.

U.S. Government Series EE or HH bonds offer a tax deferral. The interest earned each year need not be reported and will not be taxed until the bond is surrendered. If these bonds are held until retirement, the tax paid on the accumulated interest most likely will be at a lower rate due to your reduced taxable income. The interest paid on these bonds compares favorably with similar types of investments.

In some cases, deferred compensation agreements with employers may be advantageous, especially if interest is paid on the deferral. If you anticipate that you will be in a lower tax bracket after retirement and that you will be able to live comfortably on the reduced take-home income, this is a viable option. You also need to consider whether the employer will be strong enough financially in the future to pay you the deferred compensation. Deferred compensation agreements can be an excellent way of accumulating funds for retirement, but you must be cautious.

In addition, you can purchase single-premium whole-life insurance, variable life, universal life, and fixed and variable annuities. The features and benefits of these types of vehicles were discussed in Chapter 5.

REALLOCATION OF ASSETS

Reallocation of assets can help close the gap of excess retirement expenses over income. You can sell personal assets, such as fine art, property, coin collections, yachts, or vacation property, and invest the proceeds in income-producing property. If you sell unimproved land or non-dividend-paying stocks, you can invest the proceeds in income-generating investments. You can sell these assets after you retire, but don't overlook them in planning your retirement income.

SUMMARY

Accumulating savings in various types of tax-advantageous investments, savings, and pension plans will help you meet your retirement goals. These vehicles are funded with pre-tax dollars, and their tax-deferred status allows the retirement fund to increase faster.

Fig. 7-1 (Page 1 of 2)

Estimated Retirement Income and Expenses

	Spouse #1	Spouse #2
Estimated Annual Retirement Income		
Interest	$ _____	$ _____
Dividends	_____	_____
Annuities	_____	_____
Employer's Retirement Plans	_____	_____
Social Security	_____	_____
Other	_____	_____
Total Income	$ _____	$ _____

Estimated Annual Retirement Expenses		
Housing	$ _____	$ _____
Utilities and Telephone	_____	_____
Property Taxes and Insurance	_____	_____
Food and Supplies	_____	_____
Clothing	_____	_____
Transportation (include car payments)	_____	_____
Travel and Entertainment	_____	_____
Taxes	_____	_____
Medical and Dental	_____	_____
Insurance: Life, Health, Disability	_____	_____
Contributions	_____	_____

Fig. 7-1 (Page 2 of 2)

Savings and Investment   _____   _____

Miscellaneous   _____   _____

     Total Expenses $ _____ $ _____

**Difference between Income and
Expenses** $ _____ $ _____

Fig. 7-2 (Page 1 of 2)

Estimated Retirement Income and Expenses

Estimated Annual Retirement Income	Spouse #1	Spouse #2
Interest	$ 1,000	$ _____
Dividends	200	_____
Annuities	1,000	_____
Employer's Retirement Plans	8,000	_____
Social Security	10,000	_____
Other	—0—	_____
Total Income	$ 20,200	$ _____

Estimated Annual Retirement Expenses

	Spouse #1	Spouse #2
Housing	$ 10,000	$ _____
Utilities and Telephone	2,200	_____
Property Taxes and Insurance	3,000	_____
Food and Supplies	5,000	_____
Clothing	2,000	_____
Transportation (include car payments)	1,500	_____
Travel and Entertainment	1,200	_____
Taxes	1,500	_____
Medical and Dental	2,000	_____
Insurance: Life, Health, Disability	—0—	_____
Contributions	500	_____

Fig. 7-2 (Page 2 of 2)

Savings and Investment   *1,000* _____

Miscellaneous   *2,000* _____

    Total Expenses $ *31,900* $ _____

Difference between Income and

Expenses $ *(11,700)* $ _____

Social security—about as secure as a cellophane parachute.

8

Social Security

The Government Safety Net

SOCIAL SECURITY IS THE GOVERNMENT'S WAY OF PROVIDING SOME INCOME TO you and your family when you stop working because of retirement, disability, or death, but don't count on it to replace *all* lost earnings.

Approximately nine out of ten workers in the United States are currently earning some protection under social security. Approximately one out of six persons in the country receives monthly social security checks. Over 24 million people, age 65 and over, have health insurance under Medicare. And another three million disabled people under 65 have Medicare.

WHEN TO CONTACT THE SOCIAL SECURITY OFFICE

You should get in touch with the social security office if:

- you're unable to work because of an illness or injury that is expected to last a year or more.
- you're 62 or older and plan to retire.
- you're within three months of age 65, even if you don't plan to retire.
- someone in your family dies.

- you, your spouse, or your dependent children suffer permanent kidney failure.

It is also a good idea to check your social security record every three years to make sure that earnings are being correctly reported on your account. This way, if there is an error, you can have it corrected easily. In 1983, the most recent year for which the Social Security Administration has statistics, nearly 19 million earnings reports had incorrect names or social security numbers, so earnings could not be properly credited. Five million of these reports have not yet been corrected.

You can get a form for this purpose at any social security office or by calling 1-800-937-2000. There is no charge for the service. You will receive a written statement showing your past covered earnings. If you find an error, report it immediately. The statement will also show estimated future social security retirement payments you would receive, based on past earnings and expected future earnings, plus estimates of disability and survivor's payments for which you would be eligible.

WHO GETS SOCIAL SECURITY CHECKS

Monthly social security checks go to you and/or your dependents when you retire, become severely disabled, or die. In addition, Medicare, which helps to pay the cost of health care, is available at age 65 or when a disability occurs. Social security benefits include:

- Retirement Checks—When you retire, you can start receiving retirement payments as early as age 62.

- Disability Checks—If you become severely disabled before age 65, you can receive disability payments. You are considered disabled if you have a severe physical or mental condition which prevents you from working and is expected to last for at least 12 months. Your payments can start in the sixth full month of your disability. Once payments begin, they will continue for as long as you are disabled and unable to work.

- Survivors Checks—If you die, survivors payments may go to certain members of your family. A small lump-sum payment will also be made if you have an eligible surviving widow, widower, or entitled child.

PAYMENTS TO A WORKER'S FAMILY

Social security payments are made to certain dependents of a worker who has retired, become disabled, or died. If a worker is receiving retirement or disability benefits, monthly benefits also can be made to his or her:

- unmarried children under 18 (under 19 if a full-time high school student).

- unmarried children 18 or over who were severely disabled before age 22 and who continue to be disabled.

- wife or husband age 62 or over.

- wife or husband under 62 (if she or he is caring for a child under age 16 (or disabled) who is getting a benefit based on the retired or disabled worker's earnings.

Monthly benefit payments can be made to a deceased worker's:

- unmarried children under 18 (or under 19 if a full-time high school student).

- unmarried son or daughter 18 or over who was severely disabled before age 22 and who continues to be disabled.

- surviving spouse age 60 or older.

- surviving spouse or surviving divorced parent, if caring for the worker's child under age 16 (or disabled) who is getting a benefit based on the earnings of the deceased worker.

- surviving spouse age 50 or older who becomes disabled not later than seven years after the worker's death, or within seven years after parents' benefits end.

- dependent parents age 62 or older.

Payments can also go to a divorced spouse at age 62 or over, or a surviving divorced spouse at age 60, or to a disabled surviving divorced spouse age 50 or older if the marriage lasted 10 years or more.

HOW TO BUILD UP BENEFITS

Before you or your family can receive monthly payments, you must have credit for a certain amount of work under social security. The exact amount of work credit depends on your age.

Social security credit is measured in "quarters of coverage." In 1988, employees and self-employed people received one credit of coverage for each $470 of earnings. No more than four credits can be earned in any one year. For example, if you earned $1,880 or more during 1988 you would have received the full four quarters of credit.

If you earned over $1,880 you still would have earned only four credits of coverage for 1988. That is the maximum allowed, no matter how high your earnings. The amount of earnings needed to receive a quarter of coverage will increase automatically in the future to keep pace with average wages.

Remember, if you stop working before you have earned enough credit, you cannot get social security benefits. However, the credit already earned will remain on your record, so you can add to it if you return to work.

The fact that you have enough credit only means that you or your family can receive payments. The amount of the payment will depend on your earnings over a period of years.

The following is the amount of credit you need in order to receive retirement benefits:

Age 62 to be Reached in	Quarters of Credit Needed
1988	37
1989	38
1990	39
1991 or later	40

CHOOSING RETIREMENT TIME

Several factors will influence your decision about retiring, including a company pension, your ability to keep working, and your financial situation.

Another factor to consider is, if you work past the full benefit retirement age (currently 65), your monthly social security benefit will be increased by ¼% for each month (3% for each year) that you don't receive a benefit. This additional credit also increases payments to surviving spouses.

Retirement payments can be made as early as age 62. If you begin receiving payments before age 65, however, the payments will be permanently reduced. The reduction is 20% at age 62, 13⅓% at age 63, and 6⅔% at age 64. Payment amounts are also reduced if a spouse or surviving spouse begins receiving payments before age 65.

HOW WORK AFFECTS YOUR SOCIAL SECURITY PAYMENTS

You can work after you become eligible for Social Security checks. The question is: How much can you earn and still receive payments?

If you were age 65 to 70 in 1988, for example, you could have earned up to $8,400 and received all of your benefits. If you were under 65 in 1988 you could have earned up to $5,760 and received all of your benefits. These amounts will increase slightly in subsequent years. If your earnings exceed the annual exempt amount, $1.00 of benefits will be withheld for each $2.00 of earnings above that amount. Income from savings, most investments, and insurance will not reduce the payments—only earnings from a job or business. After you reach age 70, benefits will be paid in full, regardless of how much you earn.

Under a special rule, cash payments can be made to a worker's children and their surviving mother or father provided the surviving parent worked under social security 1½ years in the 3 years before the death.

If you are disabled by blindness, you do not have to meet the requirement of recent work, but you do need credit for ¼ year of work for each year since 1950 (or the year you reached 21, if later), up to the year you become blind. A minimum of 1½ years of credit is needed.

AMOUNT OF MONTHLY PAYMENTS

The actual amount of the monthly benefit is based on your past earnings. Your earnings are averaged together, and a formula is applied to the average to determine the benefit amount.

The amount of the monthly payments changes as Congress sees fit. If you reached age 65 in 1988, your monthly retirement benefit could be as high as $838, or $1,257 with a spouse.

TAXABILITY OF SOCIAL SECURITY

Social security will be taxable if the total of one-half of your benefits, plus your adjusted gross income (see Chapter 11 for definition) and any tax-free interest (e.g., municipal bond interest), exceeds $25,000 if you are single or $32,000 if you are married and filing jointly.

If you are retiring late in the year, and if you are to receive accumulated vacation pay or sick leave, consider having all of it paid to you prior to the end of that calendar year. By doing this, you will not exceed the earnings level for the next year, so you will be able to receive all of your social security tax-free. Social security payments will not be paid in any year in which you earn above the prescribed limit from a job, and vacation and sick pay are considered job-related earnings. Note, however, that once you reach age 70, it will not matter how much you earn. You will still receive all of your social security benefits.

TIME TO START PLANNING

Go down to the social security office at least three months before your expected retirement date, and begin to learn all of the options open to you. With the millions of people paying into the system, errors are bound to arise. If you allow sufficient time prior to your retirement, any discrepancies can be cleared up, and you can avoid delays in receiving your monthly benefits.

At the same time, review your options with respect to any other pension plans in which you participate.

The pension is mightier than the sword.

9

Pension Plan Distributions

Minimizing the Bite, Maximizing the Bucks

IF YOU PARTICIPATE IN A QUALIFIED PENSION PLAN AT WORK, YOU WILL BE FACED
with several options upon your retirement:

- Option 1:   Receive all of your retirement funds in one lump sum.
- Option 2:   Receive a monthly income for the remainder of your life.
- Option 3:   Rollover the entire amount into an Individual Retirement Account (IRA).

Unfortunately, employers typically provide little more than literature that
is largely incomprehensible to the average reader. The following is a brief review of the various options. Professional guidance is suggested in deciding what
to do and when to do it.

OPTION 1: LUMP-SUM DISTRIBUTION

Under many plans you can elect to receive all of your vested funds in one
lump-sum distribution. A lump-sum distribution is a distribution, within one tax

year, of your entire balance in the plan. To qualify as a lump-sum distribution, it must have been made:

- as a result of death, and thus made to the beneficiary, or
- after age 59½ is reached, or
- as a result of separation from service, or
- after a self-employed person or an owner-employee becomes disabled.

The entire amount of the lump-sum distribution may not be subject to taxation. To determine the taxable portion of the distribution, subtract, from the amount received, the amount of contributions that you made to the plan for which you did not receive a tax benefit. The result will be the amount currently subject to taxation.

You may be eligible to compute the tax on the distribution by a special five-year averaging method. For certain individuals, 10-year averaging would apply. (The rules are complex; consult a professional.) The tax on the lump-sum distribution is computed on Form 4972, separately from the tax on the rest of your income. This form must then be attached to your Form 1040.

Averaging the distribution could reduce your tax significantly. Basically, the tax on one-fifth or one-tenth of the distribution, based on the "single" tax rate tables, is multiplied by 5 or 10. The result is the total tax owed on the lump-sum distribution.

In deciding whether or not to average, obtain Form 4972 and fill it in as indicated by the instructions. You may find that the total tax may be low enough to pay currently. You would then be free to use the remainder of the funds as you please with no further taxes due, other than the tax on any earnings derived from that principal sum.

OPTION 2: MONTHLY INCOME

If you choose to have a steady income and receive a monthly distribution for the rest of your life, the portion attributable to employer contributions will be taxable in the year received. If your total income is high enough, a portion of your social security will then be taxed as well (see Chapter 8).

If you have the option within the plan provisions, you may wish to reduce your current monthly distribution to allow your spouse to continue to receive a monthly distribution after your death. If this option is not made, the monthly distributions will cease upon your death. Give careful thought to this choice, if available.

OPTION 3: ROLLOVER INTO AN IRA

You may take all of your vested funds out of the retirement plan and roll them over into a special Individual Retirement Account known as a "Rollover IRA." By choosing this option, you will defer the tax until the time you begin to take distributions from the IRA. Distributions must begin by the time you reach age 70½.

You need not rollover the entire distribution—but only the portion rolled over will be tax-deferred. The portion you do not rollover will be taxed at ordinary rates, and if you are under age 59½, a 10% penalty on the taxable portion may apply as well. You must rollover the funds within 60 days of receipt to qualify for this tax deferral.

A Rollover IRA may be an excellent choice if you continue to receive sufficient income from other sources and expect to be in a lower tax bracket sometime in the future. Meanwhile the earnings in the Rollover IRA will continue to grow, tax-deferred.

Rollover IRAs are similar to regular IRAs with respect to the types of investments allowed (see Chapter 10).

Planning for retirement requires thought and expertise. Consult the proper professionals to be sure you are making the best choices.

10

Individual Retirement Accounts

A Smart Supplement

ONE OF THE BEST—AND MOST POPULAR—WAYS TO SUPPLEMENT YOUR RETIRE-ment savings is to contribute to your own Individual Retirement Account (IRA). The tax laws encourage the establishment of your own IRA and allow such plans favorable tax treatment:

- The money contributed is tax deductible, within limits.

- The tax on the contribution is deferred until you withdraw the funds.

- The earnings within the IRA are taxed when withdrawn, not when earned.

- The taxes ultimately paid will most likely be at a lower rate than your rate at the time of contribution (i.e., when you retire you will probably be in a lower tax bracket than during your working years).

If you withdraw IRA funds prior to reaching age 59½, you will be subject to a 10% penalty plus the tax that would apply in the year of withdrawal. Assume you had contributed $2,000 into an IRA, and the earnings over two years increased the value of the plan to $2,350. If you withdraw the funds at the end of these two years, and prior to age 59½, you will pay a penalty of $235 (10% of $2,350), plus the $2,350 will be added to your other taxable income and be subject to whatever tax bracket you are in.

So, try to plan accordingly. If you know you will need the money in two or three years after you make the contribution, don't make the contribution. Granted, it is often difficult to predict your needs of the distant future, but if you can keep the funds in the IRA for at least seven years, you will still be ahead in tax savings, even with the 10% penalty for early withdrawal. There are no waivers of the 10% penalty, but at least you have the ability to withdraw the funds in an emergency. Other than for these penalties, which hopefully you will avoid, an IRA is an excellent method of building up retirement savings.

The contribution and deductibility rules and examples below have been simplified for ease of discussion. For complete rules, consult IRS Publication 590.

CONTRIBUTION RULES

Annually, you may contribute up to $2,000 or 10% of your wages, whichever is less. If your spouse works, a similar amount can be contributed on his or her behalf. If your spouse does not work, a total of $2,250 can be contributed, to be divided in any manner between the two accounts. An IRA cannot be a joint account. If both spouses desire IRAs, they must open two separate accounts.

DEDUCTIBILITY RULES

The Tax Reform Act of 1986 significantly changed the rules regarding IRAs. No longer can everyone receive a tax deduction.

You are entitled to contribute to an IRA *and* receive a full tax deduction if you are not covered by your employer's pension plan, regardless of your total taxable income. However, if you are covered by your employer's pension plan, the deductibility of your contribution is limited. (It does *not* matter if you choose not to participate. The fact that you are *eligible,* even if only for one day in the year, is what counts.) Employer-sponsored plans include qualified pension, profit-sharing, stock bonus, and annuity plans; simplified employee pension plans; and federal, state, and local governmental plans. You are considered an active participant in a plan whether your benefits are vested (whether you have full rights to the funds) or not.

Whether you file jointly or separately, if only one spouse is covered by a pension plan, both spouses are considered covered (unless you and your spouse lived apart for the entire year), so income-level limitations would apply. Thus the spouse not covered by a plan at work is penalized by not being allowed to contribute to an IRA.

The deductibility limitations of an IRA contribution are based on modified adjusted gross income. For the purposes of this determination, modified adjusted gross income includes wages, bonuses, commissions, interest and dividend income, royalties, capital gains and losses, business income, pensions, and any other taxable income, less adjustments for such things as alimony payments, penalty on early withdrawal of savings, etc. Itemized and standard deductions are not included in this calculation.

To illustrate, assume a joint return with combined wages of $35,000, interest and dividends of $500, a gain on the sale of stock of $6,500, and a home-based small business with a net loss of $1,000. The modified adjusted gross income would be calculated as follows:

Wages	$35,000
Interest and Dividends	500
Capital Gain	6,500
Business Income (Loss)	(1,000)
Modified Adjusted Gross Income	$41,000

Based on the above, the modified adjusted gross income is $41,000, and that amount is what would be used to determine the eligibility for an IRA deduction.

Again, you may annually contribute as much as $2,000 or 10% of your wages, whichever is less. This $2,000 maximum is fully deductible if your modified adjusted gross income is less than $40,000 on a joint basis or $25,000 on a single basis. The additional $250 spousal deduction, where one spouse does not work, remains available at these income levels as well.

The deduction is phased out by $200 for each $1,000 of adjusted gross income between $40,000 and $50,000 on a joint basis, and between $25,000 and $35,000 on a single basis. For example, if you filed jointly and your modified adjusted gross income was $45,000, your maximum allowable deduction would be $1,000. For the joint $41,000 modified adjusted gross income calculated above, the deduction would be limited to $1,800.

The IRA deduction is completely phased out for modified adjusted gross income levels of $50,000 or more on a joint basis and $35,000 on a single basis. Again, these limitations only apply when you (and/or your spouse, if filing jointly), are covered by a pension plan at work. Where there is no pension plan involved, you are entitled to an IRA deduction no matter how high your income level. See FIG. 10-1 for the deductibility rules.

FIGURE 10-2 can be used to determine the amount of the IRA deduction you are entitled to, if your modified adjusted gross income is within the phase-out range. FIGURE 10-3 is an example. In 1989, John and Mary Jones, both of whom work, file a joint 1988 return. John was covered by a qualified pension plan at work during 1988. Their combined modified adjusted gross income was $46,555. Because that's between $40,000 and $50,000, they can only take a partial IRA deduction, so they intend to contribute only the maximum deductible amount.

John and Mary can each make deductible contributions of up to $690 and take an IRA deduction of up to $1,380 ($690 × 2) on their joint return. If Mary only contributes $300, John's deductible contribution is still limited to $690, and they can take a deduction of up to a total of $990 on their joint return.

Note that the amount entered on line 4 has a $200 floor. For example, if line 4 is between $1 and $200, you can still deduct $200. If the amount of line 4 is zero, however, no deduction is allowed.

Note also that the deduction cannot exceed 100% of taxable compensation for the year.

FIGURE 10-3 summarizes the IRA limitation rules.

NON-DEDUCTIBLE CONTRIBUTIONS

Even if you are not entitled to a tax deduction, you should consider making an IRA contribution anyway, because all of the income tax on IRA earnings is deferred until the funds are withdrawn. You can contribute a maximum of $2,000, or $2,250 for a spousal IRA, annually.

Instead of having, for example, $2,000 on deposit in a savings account, with the interest subject to current taxes, contribute the $2,000 to a 6% IRA, and shelter the interest from current taxes. If the savings account earns 6% interest, and you pay 25% in tax, your net earnings are only 4.5%. If the IRA pays 6%, you keep the full 6%—at least for the time being.

Keep in mind that the contribution, whether tax deductible or not, need not be made by the end of each calendar year. You have until April 15 of the following year to make the contribution, and if allowable, it would be deductible on the prior year's return. A contribution made, for example, by April 15, 1989, would be deductible, if allowable, on the 1988 income tax return.

ESTABLISHING YOUR IRA

You can choose a financial institution to handle your IRA, or you can be the trustee of a self-directed IRA. Many different institutions offer IRAs, including banks, savings and loans, insurance companies, and brokerage firms. And within each institution there are many types of investments from which to choose. As your IRA grows, you may wish to put the funds in several types of investments.

Because these savings are for your retirement, the investments you choose should generally be conservative and safe. But if, for example, you have a retirement plan at work which will meet your retirement needs, you may wish to invest some of your IRA funds in somewhat more risky ventures. However, even in this case, you should limit the high-risk investments to no more than one-third of your IRA funds, and you must review these investments at least annually.

Bank Money-Market Accounts

Bank money-market accounts are an easy choice, and there normally are minimal or no fees charged for this type of IRA. The interest earned will fluctuate with changes in the economy and will not be guaranteed.

These are very similar to savings accounts, but the interest earned will be somewhat higher than on simple passbook accounts. Most banks require a minimum account balance, generally in the range of $500 to $2,500, depending on the institution. With this type of account you can withdraw funds at any time, and without a penalty—if you rollover the funds into another IRA within 60 days.

Certificate of Deposit

Certificates of deposit (CDs) are similar to money-market accounts in that they are easy to establish and generally do not involve any fees. They let you set aside funds at a predetermined interest rate and for a predetermined period of time, and they don't require your attention until the certificate comes due. Generally, the longer the term of the certificate, the higher the interest rate. However, with shorter terms you have the flexibility to take advantage of rising interest rates. On the other hand, if rates fall, a longer term with a higher rate would have been a better choice. One-year CDs are a good compromise.

Mutual Funds

Stock and bond funds usually perform well over a long period of time and are excellent vehicles for your IRA, but review the performance records of several of these funds before making your decision. You need to determine if there are fees charged at the time of purchase and again at the time of sale. Consider investing in a *no-load fund* (a fund without such fees). The fee savings enhances the earnings performance of the fund.

Many funds are tax-exempt because they invest only in exempt government securities. This type of fund is not suitable for the IRA because the earnings of such funds are generally lower than those of taxable funds. The tax savings from exempt funds normally does not compensate for the lower yield, and you cannot take advantage of the IRA's main feature, the tax deferral.

Stocks and Bonds

A self-directed IRA allows you to manage your investment portfolio. With this type of account you purchase individual stocks and bonds when you wish, but it is your responsibility to monitor these investments. This can be quite time-consuming if you will be buying and selling frequently. Unless you have accumulated a significant amount in your IRA or want to hold onto stocks or bonds for growth, you might find self-directed accounts more trouble than they are worth.

Real Estate

Real estate investments usually require more funds than are available in an IRA. They also offer various tax benefits that you could not take advantage of with an IRA. Therefore, the direct investment of IRA funds into real estate is generally not advisable.

Some real estate limited partnerships accept IRA funds. Most of these segregate the IRA investments from the other investments, for tax purposes. This type of IRA has more risks than some of the other investments discussed. Investigate these risks before investing.

ADDITIONAL IRA RULES

Here are some additional IRA rules:

- You cannot transfer individual stocks or bonds into your IRA. You must contribute the cash and then purchase the securities.
- You cannot have life insurance, gold, silver, gems, or collectibles (such as art works or antiques) in an IRA. You may, however, invest in gold or silver coins issued by the United States, as long as the coins were minted after 1986.
- Investments with tax advantages ("tax shelters") are not suitable for an IRA. Because the IRA itself is tax-deferred, any allowable depreciation or tax credits would simply be lost.
- Investments that produce capital gains are suitable, for there no longer is a special capital gains tax exclusion. However, capital *losses* are to be avoided because the losses will produce no tax benefit as part of an IRA.

ROLLOVERS

You may withdraw all or part of the assets of an IRA and exclude the withdrawal from income if you roll it over into another IRA within 60 days after withdrawal. It is not necessary that the entire amount withdrawn be rolled over, but only the amount that is rolled over during the 60-day period will be free from current tax. Once you have made a rollover, you must wait at least one year from the date of receipt of the amount withdrawn before engaging in another rollover.

A change of trustee or custodian of an IRA is not considered a rollover (although it too is free of current taxes), and therefore the one-year limitation does not apply.

REQUIRED DISTRIBUTIONS

Although you can start withdrawing funds at age 59½, you are not required to do so until April 1st of the calendar year following the calendar year in which you reach age 70½. So, if you have sufficient income, you may want to simply have your funds grow, tax-deferred, in your IRA until you are required to begin withdrawals.

SUMMARY

An individual who begins to contribute $2,000 a year into a 7% IRA at age 35 can retire at age 65 with an IRA of $202,140.

IRAs are a great way to enhance your retirement. Try to make a contribution each year, but be conservative in your investment strategy.

IRA Deductibility Rules

If You Are Covered by a Retirement Plan at Work and Your Filing Status Is

If Your Modified Adjusted Gross Income Is		• Single, or • Head of Household	• Married Filing Jointly (even if your spouse is not covered by a plan at work) • Qualifying Widow(er)	• Married Filing Separatedly
At Least	**But Less Than**	**You Can Take**	**You Can Take**	**You Can Take**
$-0-	$10,000	Full Deduction	Full Deduction	Partial Deduction
$10,000	$25,001	Full Deduction	Full Deduction	No Deduction
$25,001	$35,000	Partial Deduction	Full Deduction	No Deduction
$35,000	$40,001	No Deduction	Full Deduction	No Deduction
$40,001	$50,000	No Deduction	Partial Deduction	No Deduction
$50,000	or over	No Deduction	No Deduction	No Deduction

If You Are Not Covered by a Retirement Plan at Work and Your Filing Status Is

If Your Modified Adjusted Gross Income Is		• Married Filing Jointly (and your spouse is covered by a plan at work)	• Single, or • Head of Household	• Married Filing Jointly or Separately (and your spouse is not covered by a plan at work) • Qualifying Widow(er)	• Married Filing Separately (even if your spouse is covered by a plan at work)
At Least	**But Less Than**	**You Can Take**	**You Can Take**	**You Can Take**	**You Can Take**
$-0	$10,000	Full Deduction	Full Deduction	Full Deduction	Partial Deduction
$10,000	$25,001	Full Deduction	Full Deduction	Full Deduction	No Deduction
$25,001	$35,000	Full Deduction	Full Deduction	Full Deduction	No Deduction
$35,000	$40,001	Full Deduction	Full Deduction	Full Deduction	No Deduction
$40,001	$50,000	Partial Deduction	Full Deduction	Full Deduction	No Deduction
$50,000	or over	No Deduction	Full Deduction	Full Deduction	No Deduction

Fig. 10-2

Calculation of Maximum Partial Deduction

If FIG. 10-1 indicates you may only take a partial deduction and
your filing status is:

	Enter on Line 1:
Single, or Head of Household	$35,000
Married-joint return, or Qualifying widow(er)	$50,000
Married-separate return	$10,000

1. Amount from above $ _____

2. Modified adjusted gross income   _____

3. Subtract Line 2 from Line 1 $ _____

4. Multiply Line 3 by 20% (.20). If the result is not
    a multiple of $10, round it to the next highest
    multiple of $10 (for example, $611.40 is rounded
    to $620). If the result is less than $200, but
    more than zero, enter $200. **Maximum partial
    deduction:** $ _____

Fig. 10-3

Calculation of Maximum Partial Deduction

If FIG. 10-1 indicates you may only take a partial deduction and
your filing status is:

	Enter on Line 1:
Single, or Head of Household	$35,000
Married-joint return, or Qualifying widow(er)	$50,000
Married-separate return	$10,000

1. Amount from above $ _50,000_

2. Modified adjusted gross income   _46,555_

3. Subtract Line 2 from Line 1 $ _3,455_

4. Multiply Line 3 by 20% (.20). If the result is not
    a multiple of $10, round it to the next highest
    multiple of $10 (for example, $611.40 is rounded
    to $620). If the result is less than $200, but
    more than zero, enter $200. **Maximum partial
    deduction:** $ _690_

The average citizen works 70 days a year to earn enough money
to pay his taxes, and he does it because he loves his country,
is patriotic, and can't figure a way of getting out of them.

11

Tax Planning

Keeping Your Taxes to a Minimum

THE GOAL OF EFFECTIVE TAX PLANNING IS TO LEGALLY MINIMIZE YOUR INCOME
taxes. To reach this goal you must be aware of the laws and be able to make
an intelligent decision about the timing and method of reporting income and claiming
deductions. For the majority of taxpayers, who compute their federal income
tax on a calendar-year basis, the opportunity for tax planning ends each December 31st. As of January 1st, it is too late to engage in any planning for the previous year, except for IRA contributions, which can be made through April 15th.
Significant tax savings will depend on your taking action prior to year's end. However, no single action will be helpful for all taxpayers.

WHAT IS TAX PLANNING?

The tax law provides you with a choice of methods for reporting income and
claiming deductions. Through tax planning you can determine which methods will
reduce your tax.

When possible, income should fall into the lowest-tax-rate years, and deductions should be taken in the higher-rate years. For example, if you expect to
be in a lower tax bracket next year, you would want to defer income until then
and accelerate deductions into the current (higher-tax) year. (Remember, if you
can delay a tax you will also create for yourself an interest-free loan on the amount
of the postponed tax.) If your tax bracket will be going up, you will want the

income currently, and should put off the deductions until the following year(s).

The 1986 Tax Reform Act substantially increased the standard deduction and significantly reduced the number of brackets that a taxpayer can fall into. This makes it less likely that your bracket will change from one year to the next, and even less likely that you will be able to change your bracket by accelerating or deferring deductions. In fact, many more people will be claiming the standard deduction because of its high level and the increasingly tighter limitations on itemized deductions. Therefore, many of the tax planning techniques discussed in this chapter apply primarily to those persons who still itemize.

Economic and financial factors generally should outweigh the tax factors in year-end planning. If deferring income decreases the likelihood of ever receiving that income, deferral would not make sense.

ESTIMATING YOUR INCOME TAX

The tax system is quite complex and, despite recent "reforms," continues to become even more so. The basic premise, however, is fairly simple. All income, except for gifts, inheritances, tax-free interest, and various employee benefits, is generally considered part of gross taxable income. Once you determine your gross income there are various adjustments and exemptions, plus you have a choice of itemizing your deductions or taking the standard amount provided.

After subtracting your deductions and exemptions from your gross income you arrive at your taxable income. You then determine your tax by referring to the appropriate tax table. There are four tax tables: single, head of household, married filing jointly, and married filing separately. Your marital and dependent status on the last day of the year determines which tax table is applicable.

If you are involved in complex tax transactions, you will need the services of a professional tax preparer or advisor. However, for the majority of taxpayers, the above approach will suffice in estimating your tax for planning purposes.

Use FIGS. 11-1 AND 11-2 to estimate your federal tax. Refer to the Appendices for those items which are taxable, nontaxable, deductible, and nondeductible.

FIGURE 11-3, an example of how to use FIG. 11-1, assumes the following:

- Year of estimate: 1988
- Married couple with two children, ages 5 and 9
- Wages, salaries, etc,: $45,000
- Interest and dividends: $500
- No capital gains or losses
- Lottery winnings: $500

- Estimated loss on limited real estate partnership: $1,000
- Medical and dental expenses: $1,200
- State income taxes: $1,000
- Real estate taxes: $500
- Charitable contributions: $500
- Mortgage interest: $2,200
- Other interest: $1,200
- Miscellaneous deductions: $1,200

TAX STRATEGIES

Once you have computed your estimated tax liability, you will have a starting point from which to make some decisions. The following strategies should be considered prior to the end of each year.

State Taxes. The final installment of your estimated state income tax is normally due on January 15th of the following year. However, a prepayment by December 31st will generate an immediate federal tax deduction. So, by making the payment to the state 15 days earlier, you receive an immediate benefit, instead of waiting to receive your deduction when you file the following year's tax return.

Real Estate Taxes. A payment of the second installment of your real estate taxes by December 31st will generate an immediate deduction. Instead of waiting for the normal April 10th due date (many states use this date for the second installment), move up your payment by 3½ months, and receive the benefits immediately.

Medical Expenses. There is a medical expense exclusion of 7½% of your adjusted gross income. Although incurring medical expenses will, in many instances, not be discretionary, there are routine medical expenses that may be deferred or accelerated without any serious health consequences. If you anticipate needing this type of medical care, you may want to delay or accelerate expenses in order to "bunch" the expenses into one tax year and thus exceed the 7½% floor. For example, if your adjusted gross income is $30,000, you may deduct only those medical expenses in excess of $2,250. Therefore, in this example, the bunching of medical expenses into the current year might allow for some type of medical deduction.

Keep in mind that medical expenses are only deductible in the year they are *paid*. The fact that a bill was received is not sufficient. If a credit card is used to pay medical expenses, the deduction is allowable in the year charged even though the credit card bill may not be paid until the following year.

Charitable Contributions. Charitable contributions are deductible in the year they are made. If you write a check to a charitable organization on December 31st, you receive a deduction in the current year even if the charity receives and cashes the check the following year. So, if you need to maximize your deductions for the current year, you might, for example, consider making advance payments on future pledges to your alma mater.

You must itemize your deductions to claim a charitable contribution. If you claim the standard deduction, you can no longer claim a charitable deduction. This change, enacted with the 1986 Tax Act, reduces the tax benefit of a contribution deduction, because more people will be claiming the new higher standard deduction.

Lump-Sum Pension Distributions. If you are retiring from active employment this year or next, it may be important to have your employer pay the total benefit from a qualified retirement plan within one tax year. This allows you to calculate the tax on the lump-sum payment by a special averaging method, and will generally result in a lower tax.

If you worked during most of the current year you may wish to delay your retirement and the receipt of your benefits until the following year in order to spread out the tax effect.

Recipients of a lump-sum distribution from a qualified retirement plan have the option of rolling the payment over into an IRA, tax-deferred, within 60 days of receipt. The tax is simply postponed until the year you withdraw the money from the IRA. The entire proceeds need not be rolled over to qualify for this tax deferral. You may wish to keep a portion of the distribution, pay the tax on it currently, and roll the remainder into the IRA. For additional information, see Chapter 10.

Annual Bonus, Commission, or Pending Contract. If you expect a year-end bonus from your employer, and do not expect to be in a higher bracket next year, have the bonus paid in January (January 2nd is fine) instead of December. This will shift the income, and thus the tax, out of the current year. The same would be true for commissions and other fees. Similarly, if you refrain from completing sales, contracts, or construction jobs (or accepting professional fees or royalties) until the first of the following year, you can make a substantial difference. Accepting fees, commissions, or bonuses on December 31st means an immediate federal and state tax. By waiting a few days, until January 2nd or so, the federal and state taxes will be postponed for a full year.

Interest Payments. Interest on personal loans, auto loans, and credit card interest becomes nondeductible after a five-year phase-out period which began in 1987. If you paid this type of interest in 1988, only 40% will be deductible;

for 1989, 20%; for 1990, 10%; and beginning in 1991, there will be no deduction. So, try to reduce these types of loans.

The deductibility rules for interest on home equity loans have also changed. Generally the interest expense incurred is fully deductible. However, for loans made between August 16, 1987, through October 12, 1987, the interest is fully deductible only if the loan does not exceed the purchase price of the home plus the cost of any improvements, except where the loan proceeds are used for medical or educational purposes (in which case the interest will be fully deductible to the extent that the loan does not exceed the fair market value of the home).

For loans made October 13, 1987 or later, the rules change again. Additional home-equity financing can't exceed the cost of the home plus improvements by more than $100,000. However, the proceeds can be used for any purpose and are not limited to medical or educational expenses. Any debt in excess of the $100,000 maximum is considered personal debt and is subject to the phase-out rules.

IRAs. You can make a contribution to an IRA up until April 15th and receive the deduction for the prior tax year. So you can decide at the time your return is prepared (assuming that it is before April 15th) if the IRA will produce a tax savings.

If you are due to receive a refund, you may wish to file your return early, January or February, and hopefully receive the refund prior to April 15th when the IRA contribution is due.

Retirement Plan for the Self-Employed. If you have net earnings from self-employment, you may be eligible to open and contribute to a Keogh plan. Refer back to Chapter 7 for the details.

U.S. Savings Bonds, CDs, and T-Bills. As a cash-basis taxpayer you have a choice in reporting the interest earned on U.S. savings bonds. You can report the annual increase in value currently, or defer the taxes until you redeem the bonds. By recognizing a small amount of income each year, as opposed to a large sum all in one year, you may reduce your overall tax bite.

The purchase of certain short-term CDs towards year-end will defer current year's accrued interest income until the following year. The CD must be the type on which interest is not credited, nor made available without substantial penalties, before the maturity date the following year. Treasury bills also offer a similar opportunity for deferral because the interest is generally not recognized as income until the security is redeemed. In addition, T-bill and savings bond interest is not subject to state and local income taxes.

Often-Overlooked Deductions. Total miscellaneous deductions must exceed 2% of adjusted gross income to be deductible. Consider the following, which may help you exceed this exclusion:

- Tax preparation fees are deductible, as are legal expenses for certain tax planning and negotiation of employment contracts. Have your attorney itemize the bill indicating the amount attributable to tax planning incident to estate planning or divorce, or the time spent on an employment contract. If your attorney does not break down the bill, you will not be entitled to a deduction, because estate planning and divorce work per se are nondeductible items. However, the tax planning related to these matters is fully deductible.

- Professional dues and publications are deductible.

- Safe deposit box fees are deductible if used to store investments such as stock certificates and bonds.

- Business gift expenses are deductible up to $25 per recipient.

- Telephone, postage, office supplies, and publications related to investment activities or the determination of your tax liability are deductible. Also, don't forget the cost of receiving your daily newspaper; it's deductible even if your investment activities are minimal.

- Expenses for education that *don't* qualify you for a new job are deductible. Amounts paid to employment agencies for assistance in finding a job are deductible as well.

- To the extent a home computer is used for business or investment purposes, the costs associated with that use, including depreciation, are deductible. However, you must keep a diary of the business use of the computer.

- You can deduct custodial fees paid by you to a custodian or trustee of your IRA. This deduction is permitted in addition to the maximum IRA contribution or deduction, but pay the fee separately —not out of the already-contributed IRA funds.

- Courts have even indicated that attaché cases used in a business, as well as seasonal greeting cards mailed to clients and customers, are deductible.

- Travel expenses, including transportation, food, and lodging, related to the inspection or maintenance of investment properties are also deductible.

- Only 80% of business meal and entertainment expenses are deductible, and that amount is subject to the 2% overall floor on all miscellaneous deductions. You must keep good records and receipts, business must be discussed, and the expense cannot be extravagant.

For additional deductions, see Appendix B.

To paraphrase Mark Twain—like the weather, everybody talks about income tax, but nobody does anything about it. Now, it's up to you!

Fig. 11-1

Federal Tax Planning Worksheet

INCOME
  Wages, salary, bonuses, commission $ _____
  Interest and dividends   _____
  Net capital gain (loss)   _____
  Other income (alimony received, fees, etc.)   _____
  Limited partnerships (40% of net loss in 1988,
    20% in 1989, 10% in 1990, and 0% in 1991)   _____
        Gross Income $ _____
LESS: ADJUSTMENTS
  IRA payment (if allowable)   (_____)
  Keogh contribution   (_____)
  Alimony paid   (_____)
        Total Adjustments   (_____)
        ADJUSTED GROSS INCOME $ _____
ITEMIZED DEDUCTIONS
  Medical and dental (above 7.5% of adjusted
    gross income) $ _____
  State income taxes   _____
  Real estate taxes   _____
  Charitable contributions   _____
  Interest expenses
    First and second homes   _____
    Personal loans, auto loans and credit cards
    (40% allowed in 1988, 20% in 1989
    10% in 1990, and 0% in 1991)   _____
  Miscellaneous deductions and employee business
    expenses (above 2% of adjusted gross income)   _____
        Total Itemized Deductions $ _____
LESS: TOTAL DEDUCTIONS (larger of total itemized
  deductions or standard deduction: $5,000 joint,
  $3,000 single, $4,400 head of household)   (_____)
LESS: PERSONAL EXEMPTIONS ($1,950 each in 1988,
  $2.000 in 1989)   (_____)

    TAXABLE INCOME $ _____

    FEDERAL INCOME TAX (from FIG. 11-2) $ _____

Fig. 11-2

FEDERAL TAX TABLE*

(1988 Tax Year)

Filing Status	Taxable Income	Tax Rate
Single	$0 to $17,850 Excess over $17,850	15% 28%
Married Filing Jointly or Qualifying Widow(er)	$0 to $29,750 Excess over $29,750	15% 28%
Married Filing Separately	$0 to $14,875 Excess over $14,875	15% 28%
Head of Household	$0 to $23,900 Excess over $23,900	15% 28%

*These rates in this table are simplified for the purposes of estimation.

Fig. 11-3 (Page 1 of 2)

Federal Tax Planning Worksheet

INCOME	
Wages, salary, bonuses, commission	$ 45,000
Interest and dividends	500
Net capital gain (loss)	-o-
Other income (alimony received, fees, etc.)	500
Limited partnerships (40% of net loss in 1988, 20% in 1989, 10% in 1990, and 0% in 1991)	400[a]
Gross Income	$ 46,400
LESS: ADJUSTMENTS	
IRA payment (if allowable)	(-o-)
Keogh contribution	(-o-)
Alimony paid	(-o-)
Total Adjustments	(-o-)
ADJUSTED GROSS INCOME	$ 46,400
ITEMIZED DEDUCTIONS	
Medical and dental (above 7.5% of adjusted gross income)	$ -o-[b]
State income taxes	1,000
Real estate taxes	500
Charitable contributions	500
Interest expenses	
First and second homes	2,200
Personal loans, auto loans and credit cards (40% allowed in 1988, 20% in 1989 10% in 1990, and 0% in 1991)	480[c]
Miscellaneous deductions and employee business expenses (above 2% of adjusted gross income)	272[d]
Total Itemized Deductions	$ 4,952
LESS: TOTAL DEDUCTIONS (larger of total itemized deductions or standard deduction: $5,000 joint, $3,000 single, $4,400 head of household)	(5,000[e])
LESS: PERSONAL EXEMPTIONS ($1,950 each in 1988, $2.000 in 1989)	(7,800)

Fig. 11-3 (Page 2 of 2)

TAXABLE INCOME $ _33,600_

FEDERAL INCOME TAX (from FIG. 11-2) $ _5,541_[f]

Notes:

[a] The loss of $1,000 is limited to 40% in 1988; $1,000 × 40% = $400.

[b] Adjusted gross income of $46,400 × 7.5% = $3,480. Medical expenses are $1,200; thus there is no deduction as the amount does not exceed the floor of $3,480.

[c] Other interest of $1,200 is limited to 40% in 1988; $1,200 × 40% = $480.

[d] Adjusted gross income of $46,400 × 2% = $928. Miscellaneous deductions = $1,200 which are then reduced by the $928, and the allowed deduction is the difference, $272 ($1,200 − $928 = $272).

[e] Total itemized deductions = $4,952; however, the standard deduction allowed for married filing jointly is $5,000. Therefore, the $5,000 is claimed.

[f] The table for married filing jointly is used.

12

Investment Strategies

Risk vs. Reward

THE GOAL OF THIS BOOK IS TO INCREASE YOUR ACCUMULATED CAPITAL. BUT THE
mere fact that you have set aside funds for savings is not sufficient. These funds
need to be invested wisely so they can grow. The numerous investment strategies available, from simple savings accounts to complex investment vehicles, come
with various risk factors. The greater the risk of losing your money, the greater
the potential return. Before embarking on an investment strategy it is important
to plan and become knowledgeable of the investment choices available.

INVESTMENT OBJECTIVES

Your investment objectives will vary depending on your particular needs,
financial position, and preferences. Consider the following important investment
characteristics.

Safety. Is the investment safe? Will I get my money back? Will I really earn
the amount projected? These are questions typically asked. To many people,
positive answers to these questions are required before they will invest. For
these conservative investors, savings accounts, CDs, money-market funds, U.S.
Treasury bills, and government savings bonds are available. These are very,
very, low-risk investments in which the security of the principal is virtually assured.

Liquidity. Many investors look for liquidity—they want to be able to turn their investments into cash quickly, in case they need the funds for a purchase or some other purpose. Everyone should have some liquid investments for emergencies, even if they represent only a small portion of the total investment portfolio. Savings accounts, CDs, money-market funds, and Treasury bills provide such liquidity.

Overall Increase in Value. Capital accumulation, the overall increase in value of the principal sum invested, is a goal of most investors. To experience true growth, your return on investment must exceed the inflation rate. If the inflation rate in a given year is 5%, your investments must grow in excess of 5% that year. If they do not exceed the inflation rate, you will experience a loss. Stocks, bonds, and savings accounts rarely exceed high inflation rates, but real estate and precious metals frequently do. Therefore, a mixed growth portfolio is important. A portfolio comprised partially of stocks, bonds, and/or savings accounts, and partially of real estate and/or precious metals, is advisable. This way, if inflation rates change, you will be protected by at least some of your investments.

Cash Flow. A steady income from an investment is of utmost importance to many people, especially those approaching retirement who want to supplement their retirement income.

Income-generating investments include stocks that pay high dividends (e.g., most utility stocks), corporate and municipal bonds or bond funds, mutual funds specializing in income generation, Treasury bills, and CDs.

RISK OF LOSS

The risk of loss is always of concern. There are various risks an investor must be aware of.

Price Fluctuations. The price of an investment may vary as economic trends change. During a so-called "bull market," stock prices generally rise, while in a "bear market," prices generally fall. Such fluctuations can occur rapidly due to news events or the world economic situation. Who ever expected the bull market that was so strong in the mid-1980s to turn around so completely on October 19, 1987, now known as "Black Monday"? There is *always* a risk that an investment will fall from its purchase price.

Internal Problems. There also is always a risk that problems will arise within a company or investment venture. Faulty products, lawsuits, or product obsolescence may have a severe effect on the price of a stock.

Interest Rate Changes. Stocks, bonds, and real estate are all affected by rising and falling interest rates.

Inflation. If an investment's rate of growth does not exceed the inflation rate, there is a strong possibility that the value or selling price of the investment will decrease. Long-term fixed-income investments are especially sensitive to inflation-rate fluctuations.

TYPES OF INVESTMENTS

Discussed below are some of the most popular types of investments. For a more comprehensive list, refer to FIG. 12-1.

Common Stock

Certificates of common stock represent ownership of the outstanding capital of a corporation. Each share of common stock entitles the owner to one vote within the corporation. The value of common stock can fluctuate greatly depending on the profits of the corporation, its future income and growth potential, new technology, the world economic and political situation, interest rates, inflation, etc. Therefore, common stock ownership can be subject to a great deal of risk.

Some common stocks are considered *growth-oriented* and will never pay a dividend. Others are *income-oriented* and pay regular dividends.

Prior to investing in common stock, be sure to research the issuing corporation and learn as much as possible about its earnings and growth, both in the past and projections for the future. Most stock brokers can provide such information.

Preferred Stock

When a corporation is liquidated, the initial cash goes toward paying off the general creditors. If funds remain, the holders of preferred stock receive a distribution, and if funds still remain, the common stockholders receive a distribution.

Although dividends are generally not guaranteed, preferred stockholders receive current and past unpaid dividends before common stockholders. If a preferred stock is issued with, for example, a 6% dividend rate stated, no dividends can be paid to the common stockholders until the preferred stockholders receive their 6%.

A disadvantage is that the issuer may *call in* (buy back) preferred stock, but a corporation normally will do this only if the preferred dividend rate is higher than current interest rates. An investor, in this case, could lose a high-yield investment.

Bonds

A bond represents a debt of a corporation or municipality. The interest on a bond is fixed-rate and is paid at regular intervals. If the bond is held until its maturity date, the entire *face value* will be paid.

During the period prior to the maturity date (sometimes 20 or 30 years), the value of the bond may fluctuate due to changes in interest rates. If interest rates fall below the bond rate, the bond becomes more valuable and its price increases. When interest rates exceed the bond rate, the bond's value decreases. The value of a bond may also decrease when the issuing entity, whether a corporation or municipality, faces financial problems—i.e., when the likelihood of the face value being repaid on the maturity date decreases.

Note that, with respect to bonds issued by states and municipalities, the interest is usually exempt from federal income tax. In many cases, the interest on a state's bonds will be exempt from that state's income tax as well.

Zero Coupon Bonds. Zero coupon bonds have become popular in recent years. This type of bond pays no interest until the maturity date. Accordingly, it is sold at a large discount. For example, you may pay $250 for a bond which will mature 15 to 20 years later at a value of $1,000. Interest on zero coupon bonds is taxable on an annual basis, except when they are tax-exempt municipal bonds or they are purchased in a tax-deferred retirement plan, such as an IRA.

Mortgage-Backed Securities

Mortgage-backed securities are issued to finance large numbers of real estate mortgages. These investments are usually guaranteed by the Veterans Administration (VA), Federal Housing Administration (FHA), or Government National Mortgage Association (GNMA).

"Ginnie Maes," for example, are securities whose assets are fully guaranteed by the GNMA. Although the principal is guaranteed, and the interest rate is fixed, if market interest rates rise above the Ginnie Mae's rate, the market value of the security decreases, so these securities are not risk-free.

Funds

Money-market funds invest entirely in debt instruments which mature in one year or less (i.e., CDs or U.S. Treasury bills). These funds bear very little risk; they are very safe investments. The yield (earnings) on such funds varies on a daily basis, as interest rates fluctuate.

Mutual funds typically invest in common stocks, bonds, or both. Many of these funds have stated objectives, e.g., growth, income, high risk, etc. The risk of a major loss in a mutual fund is lessened because the investments within the fund's portfolio are diversified.

Real Estate

Real estate investments may take many different forms—direct investments, partnerships, joint ventures, and others. The property involved may be raw land, commercial property, or residential rental.

Real estate affords an opportunity for higher growth and appreciation than is likely with other types of investments. It also offers some tax advantages, though the Tax Reform Act of 1986 took many of the benefits away. It is very common to borrow when buying real estate. This allows you to invest in higher-value properties than you could otherwise afford.

Keep in mind that real estate investments are generally growth investments. They do not produce much income or cash flow, and should not be considered liquid.

Oil and Gas

Oil and gas investments are widely known as high-risk ventures. Exploratory ventures (oil or gas searches) involve the highest risk. Ventures that drill near successful wells, known as developmental ventures, are somewhat less risky. Currently-producing wells involve the least risk.

The overall risk with these ventures is the fluctuating price of oil, which in the past few years has varied from a high of $30 per barrel to a low of $8 per barrel. But there are many advantages, again reduced by tax reform, which continue to make such investments attractive.

Tax Shelters

Tax shelters are investments that legally provide you with a reduction of your current income taxes—they "shelter" your current income from tax. Many types of investments have tax advantages that allow them to be classified as shelters. If you have an IRA or pension plan, you already have one type of shelter.

If you are considering investing in a tax shelter, you need to consider both the tax and the non-tax aspects of the investment. A shelter that offers the potential of large tax savings may also carry a high risk that the entire investment could be lost. With careful attention to all the risks and benefits, however, your investment may be successful.

The federal government is no longer as generous a benefactor in speculative investment activities as it once was. Just a few years ago, investors who into tax shelters, such as oil drilling ventures, found that the government absorbed most of the risk. The top tax rate on unearned income, 70%, meant that if the oil well came up dry, the investor lost 30 cents on the dollar, at most. Then they went to a 50-50 split. But under the new tax rules, the brunt of the risk shifts to you, the investor. The top rate of 33% means that 67% of the risk is yours.

Precious Metals

Investment in precious metals, such as gold, platinum, or silver, provides a hedge against inflation and diversity in an investment portfolio. But precious metals are high-risk investments. Their value can fluctuate greatly. The world economic and political situation, interest rates, inflation rates, and currency fluctuations all affect the value of precious metals. Note that, in addition to owning coins or bullion outright, specialized mutual funds are available.

Insurance

Insurance was never considered much of an investment vehicle until recently. Insurance companies are now offering products which can be added to an investment portfolio. Single-premium whole life insurance and universal life insurance are such products; they offer many tax advantages which add to their investment appeal. For a more detailed discussion of insurance products, review Chapter 5.

YOUR *10% OFF THE TOP* FUND

Let your *10% Off the Top* fund accumulate in your savings account until it reaches $2,500 or $3,000. Then begin to consider other investment vehicles for this and any other funds you may have accumulated. As stated previously, your goal is to achieve reasonable asset growth. In addition, you will want to have a good balance of (1) investment risk vs. investment yield and (2) liquid vs. non-liquid investments.

Your age will have a great bearing on the relative importance of these objectives. As you grow older you will want to reduce risks, increase liquidity, and have a higher percentage of income-oriented investments. This is because you have less time to recover from major financial downturns as you grow older and you will want more liquid assets and income-oriented investments to supplement your retirement income.

On the other hand, a younger investor will want an entirely different mix in his or her investment portfolio. Asset growth and wealth accumulation will be the important objectives.

The amount of assets available for investment will have a bearing on your investment decisions as well. Savings accounts can be opened easily and for small amounts. Higher-rate accounts usually have minimums of a few hundred to several thousand dollars. Also, some investments that can be obtained in small denominations will be impractical because the fees or commissions are too high.

You need to determine what *your* investment goals are. You might want to split your available assets—invest 50% in relatively risk-free liquid investments and the other 50% in somewhat more risky non-liquid ventures. Another method would be to have one-third in safe liquid investments, one-third in moderately risky ventures, and one-third in high-risk/high-potential investments. But, if you go this route, be prepared to lose the entire one-third invested in high-risk ventures. I recommend that you stay away from high risk. Stick to the low and moderate-risk ventures. You may win big with high risk, but you could also lose big.

Fig. 12-1 (Page 1 of 2)

INVESTMENT OPTIONS

Low-Risk Investments

Money-Market Funds   Certificates of Deposit (CDs)
Savings Accounts   U.S. Treasury Bills
NOW Account   Tax-Exempt Money-Market Funds

Stocks

Common: Preferred:
  Growth   Convertible into Common Stock
  Income

Bonds

Corporate: U.S. Government:
  Convertible into Common Stock   U.S. Savings Bonds
  Zero Coupon   Treasury Notes and Bonds

                                    Mortgage-Backed securities:
                                        Ginnie Mae
Municipal: Fannie Mae
  General Obligation (general revenue-raising, not tied to any specific project)
  Limited Obligation (issued to fund a specific project, e.g., schools, etc.)
  Zero Coupon

Mutual Funds

Growth   International Companies
Maximum-Growth / High-Risk   Small Companies / Higher-Risk
Balanced-Growth and Income   Bonds
Income   Municipal Bonds

Fig. 12-1 (Page 2 of 2)

Real Estate

Direct Ownership   Partnership   Joint Venture

Oil and Gas

Partnership   Working Interest   Royalty Interest

Collectibles

Antiques   Gems
Art   Stamps
Coins

Precious Metals

Gold   Silver   Platinum

Insurance Products

Universal Life   Single-Premium Whole Life

Others

Tax Shelters   Annuities   Commodities

Benjamin Franklin wrote, " . . . in this world nothing is certain but death and taxes." What taxpayers resent is they don't come in that order.

13

Estate Planning

Leave Less to the Government

THE PURPOSE OF PLANNING YOUR ESTATE IS TO ENSURE, TO THE EXTENT POSSIBLE, that your wishes are carried out at your death. A properly drafted and executed will is paramount to meeting your objectives, which will include the minimization of death taxes, settlement of debts, direction of the distribution of your assets, and provision for survivors.

Use the following comments and recommendations only as a guide to the alternatives available to you. Consult your legal and tax advisors when appropriate. Your will (and any trust document) should be drafted by qualified legal counsel.

A review of all the estate planning tools available is beyond the scope of this book. Instead, I will emphasize a few key areas.

FEDERAL ESTATE TAX

After your death, federal estate tax is imposed on the net worth of your estate. Your estate's assets include real property (residence and rental property), partnerships, sole proprietorships, stocks, bonds, tax shelters, insurance proceeds, and personal effects. Your liabilities and certain allowable expenses (i.e., funeral expenses, administration and probate expenses, etc.) are subtracted from your assets to arrive at your estate's net worth.

Under current tax law you may pass 100% of your assets to your surviving spouse tax-free. And if your estate is $600,000 or less, it will not be subject to any federal estate tax under current law, regardless of who receives the assets. If your estate exceeds $600,000 there are many opportunities to reduce your federal estate tax. You should review these with your advisor.

Besides the federal estate tax, many states impose a tax as well. A check of the rules in your particular state is advisable. If you relocate to another state, and your estate is sizeable, learn about the rules beforehand. The tax situation can make quite a difference.

WILLS

If you have property of more than nominal value, if you are married, or if you have children, you need a will. When you have a will, *you* determine who will inherit your property. When you don't have a will, the state decides. State formulas for distributing assets generally favor close relatives. But perhaps that is not what you want. Or, for example, you may wish to leave the major portion of your estate to your spouse while most states would only designate ⅓ to ½ for the spouse. And state laws do not provide for distributions to favorite charities, friends, or distant relatives. In fact, if there are no surviving relatives, the state gets the money.

Without a will your heirs may have to incur considerable legal cost and long delays. Even worse, you will not have a say as to who will bring up your minor children if you and your spouse die in an accident. Without a will, the court chooses. Therefore, if you have children, even if you only have nominal assets, you need to have a will.

Most people find it very difficult to accept the fact that they will die. So they put the thought out of their minds; it is easier to simply put off the will than face the reality of death. Most attorneys I know haven't gotten around to drafting their own wills.

Once you decide you need a will, the process is relatively simple. In many cases it can be handled in one meeting with an attorney. The cost of a simple will is in the area of $300 to $500—a very small price for peace of mind.

After you have a will drawn up and executed, don't ignore it. Review and update it periodically.

LIVING TRUSTS

The creation of a revocable trust, known also as a *living trust*, is an essential addition to many wills.

A revocable living trust is created during your lifetime and can be amended or revoked at any time prior to death. It has no tax advantages, but there are many other reasons for creating one.

Without such a trust an estate must be settled in probate court. Attorney fees and court costs can be significant, there can be considerable delays, and the entire estate is part of the public record.

With a living trust there are no court proceedings. The assets are simply distributed according to the trust's direction, and administrative costs are minimal. Plus, the trust ensures privacy and moves the assets to the beneficiaries expeditiously (six to eight weeks is the norm). Certification of title transfers by a notary public or attorney is all that is required. Without a living trust, two or more years may pass before assets are transferred to the beneficiaries.

Another reason for creating a living trust is to avoid being placed under a court-appointed guardian should you become unable to handle your affairs. For example, if a home is in joint tenancy, a wife would be precluded from selling it if her husband became incompetent. She would be required to have a court appoint her as conservator. Then, and only then, could she sell the home. In addition, as a conservator she would be required to maintain impeccable records for the court. A living trust could avoid this problem. It could specify that the wife would manage the affairs if the husband became incompetent. Then, the courts would not intervene.

Upon the creation of a living trust, title to real estate, securities, and other assets are placed in the name of the trust (e.g., The John Q. Reader Revocable Trust) rather than in your individual name. This is done while you are alive. Generally, you are the trustee and manage the assets just as you did previously. There are no management fees or loss of control. The trust then outlines the method of distribution of assets after your death. Prior to death, the beneficiaries and distribution of assets can change at any time, and as many times during your lifetime as you desire.

As with a will, there is a fee involved, generally $300 to $400.

THE DISTRIBUTABLE ESTATE

The distributable estate is the property that will remain after payment of taxes, funeral and administration expenses, debts, and any other costs which may arise. Before you establish a will and trust you need to assess your distributable estate and determine what to leave, how to leave it, and to whom to leave it.

Keep your objectives in mind during this review of your distributable estate. Unless your estate is large, you probably will not be able to accomplish everything you might wish to. You will need to weigh your priorities and analyze your beneficiaries by weighing their needs against what you are able to provide for them.

Chapter 2 included schedules for recording your assets and liabilities. If you have completed them you may wish to refer to them as you complete FIGS. 13-1A AND 13-1B. The values you enter should be based on estimated current market value. Then determine your estimated estate costs and taxes using FIGS. 13-2A/B THROUGH 13-4.

FIGURES 13-5 AND 13-6 are examples for an estate under $600,000. FIGURES 13-7 THROUGH 13-12 are examples for an estate over $600,000.

YOUR BENEFICIARIES

You now know what is available for distribution to your beneficiaries, but the more difficult question may be, who gets what? In many cases this process is very simple. Your entire estate is left to your spouse, a child, or a friend. In some cases an even division amongst two or more beneficiaries may suffice.

In many other cases this process may not be as simple. You may need to answer these questions:

- Is the support of your spouse your main objective? Or does your spouse have a significant estate of his/her own?

- How should your children be treated? Equally? Is there a disabled child who must be treated with special attention?

- How should your grandchildren be treated?

- Do you have dependent parents that need consideration?

- Are there other relatives to consider?

- Are there gifts to charity that you would like made?

You need to carefully consider these questions and numerous others that will arise during this process. You may wish to consult other family members or your attorney and discuss the possible ramifications of your decisions.

When you make your decisions, your attorney can record them in your will and/or trust documents. Again, review these decisions at least annually, and make any changes you desire based on recent deaths, births, or other events.

When you realize how much is at stake—the well-being of your entire family and the protection of your property—you will find that estate planning requires your immediate and continued attention.

Fig. 13-1A (Page 1 of 2)

INVENTORY OF ASSETS

Spouse #1

Type of Property	Separately Owned	50% of Jointly Owned	Total
Cash:			
Checking Account	$_____	$_____	$_____
Savings Account	_____	_____	_____
Securities:			
Stocks	_____	_____	_____
Bonds	_____	_____	_____
Mutual Funds	_____	_____	_____
Receivables:			
Notes	_____	_____	_____
Mortgages	_____	_____	_____
Real Estate	_____	_____	_____
Businesses	_____	_____	_____
Residence	_____	_____	_____
Pension Plan	_____	_____	_____
Profit-Sharing Plan	_____	_____	_____
IRA	_____	_____	_____
Life Insurance:			
Personal	_____	_____	_____
Group	_____	_____	_____
Personal Property:			
Automobile	_____	_____	_____
Jewelry	_____	_____	_____
Art	_____	_____	_____

Fig. 13-1A (Page 2 of 2)

Furniture
Other Assets:

_____ _____ _____ _____

Total Value of Estate $_____ $_____ $_____

Fig. 13-1B (Page 1 of 2)

INVENTORY OF ASSETS

Spouse #2

Type of Property	Separately Owned	50% of Jointly Owned	Total
Cash:			
Checking Account	$_____	$_____	$_____
Savings Account	_____	_____	_____
Securities:			
Stocks	_____	_____	_____
Bonds	_____	_____	_____
Mutual Funds	_____	_____	_____
Receivables:			
Notes	_____	_____	_____
Mortgages	_____	_____	_____
Real Estate	_____	_____	_____
Businesses	_____	_____	_____
Residence	_____	_____	_____
Pension Plan	_____	_____	_____
Profit-Sharing Plan	_____	_____	_____
IRA	_____	_____	_____
Life Insurance:			
Personal	_____	_____	_____
Group	_____	_____	_____
Personal Property:			
Automobile	_____	_____	_____
Jewelry	_____	_____	_____
Art	_____	_____	_____

Fig. 13-1B (Page 2 of 2)

Furniture
Other Assets:

Total Value of Estate $_____ $_____ $_____

Fig. 13-2A

ESTIMATED ESTATE COSTS
AND FEDERAL TAXES
Spouse #1

Total Value of Estate (from FIG. 13-1A—
separately owned plus 50% of jointly owned
property) $ _____

Deduct:

Debts $ _____

Funeral and last illness expenses[1]   _____

Income and other taxes due[2]   _____

Administration costs[3]   _____

  Total Deductions   (_____)

  Gross Estate $ _____

  Less: Federal Estate Tax[4]   (_____)

  Net Estate Available For Distribution to Beneficiaries $ _____

[1] An estimate will be required; $3,000-$5,000 should be sufficient unless a major illness is involved.
[2] Any unpaid tax liabilities should be recorded.
[3] For smaller or uncomplicated estates, $500 to $1,000 should be sufficient. Larger or more complex estates may require 5% to 10% of the estate value.
[4] If the estate is over $600,000 a tax may be due. (A schedule is provided for this calculation.) For estates under $600,000, no federal estate tax will be due.

Fig. 13-2B

ESTIMATED ESTATE COSTS AND FEDERAL TAXES

Spouse #2

Total Value of Estate (from FIG. 13-1B—
separately owned plus 50% of jointly owned
property) $ _____

Deduct:

Debts $ _____

Funeral and last illness expenses[1]   _____

Income and other taxes due[2]   _____

Administration costs[3]   _____

Total Deductions   (_____)

Gross Estate $ _____

Less: Federal Estate Tax[4]   (_____)

Net Estate Available For Distribution to Beneficiaries $ _____

---

[1] An estimate will be required; $3,000-$5,000 should be sufficient unless a major illness is involved.
[2] Any unpaid tax liabilities should be recorded.
[3] For smaller or uncomplicated estates, $500 to $1,000 should be sufficient. Larger or more complex estates may require 5% to 10% of the estate value.
[4] If the estate is over $600,000 a tax may be due. (A schedule is provided for this calculation.) For estates under $600,000, no federal estate tax will be due.

Fig. 13-3.

FEDERAL ESTATE TAX CALCULATION
(For Estates Over $600,000 In Value)

	Spouse #1	Spouse #2
Gross Estate[1]	_____	_____
Less: Marital Deduction[2]	(_____)	(_____)
Less: Contributions[3]	(_____)	(_____)
TAXABLE ESTATE	===========	===========
Federal Estate Tax[4]	_____	_____
Less: Unified Credit[5]	($192,800)	($192,800)
NET FEDERAL ESTATE TAX	===========	===========

[1] From Estimated Estate Costs and Taxes (FIG. 13-2A/B).

[2] For married couples the taxable estate is reduced by the amount bequeathed to the surviving spouse. An assumption needs to be made between Spouse #1 and Spouse #2 as to who will die first. Generally it is assumed Spouse #1 will die first and the marital deduction will therefore only apply to the calculation for Spouse #1. If the entire estate is left to the surviving spouse, there will not be any federal estate tax.

[3] Any anticipated or directed charitable contributions are to be recorded.

[4] The federal estate-tax rate schedule should be consulted.

[5] The current credit is $192,800.

Fig. 13-4

FEDERAL ESTATE TAX RATE SCHEDULE

If the taxable estate is

Over	But not over	Tax	+	%	On excess over
$ 0	$ 10,000	$ 0		18	$ 0
10,000	20,000	1,800		20	10,000
20,000	40,000	3,800		22	20,000
40,000	60,000	8,200		24	40,000
60,000	80,000	13,000		26	60,000
80,000	100,000	18,200		28	80,000
100,000	150,000	23,800		30	100,000
150,000	250,000	38,800		32	150,000
250,000	500,000	70,800		34	250,000
500,000	750,000	155,800		37	500,000
750,000	1,000,000	248,300		39	750,000
1,000,000	1,250,000	345,800		41	1,000,000
1,250,000	1,500,000	448,300		43	1,250,000
1,500,000	2,000,000	555,800		45	1,500,000
2,000,000	2,500,000	780,800		49	2,000,000
2,500,000	....	1,025,800		50	2,500,000

Fig. 13-5 (Page 1 of 2)

INVENTORY OF ASSETS

Spouse #1

$ Type of Property	Separately Owned	50% of Jointly Owned	Total
Cash:			
Checking Account	$ —0—	2,000	$ 2,000
Savings Account	—0—	10,000	10,000
Securities:			
Stocks	5,000	10,000	15,000
Bonds	—0—	—0—	—0—
Mutual Funds	—0—	5,000	5,000
Receivables:			
Notes	—0—	—0—	—0—
Mortgages	—0—	—0—	—0—
Real Estate	—0—	80,000	80,000
Businesses	—0—	—0—	—0—
Residence	—0—	100,000	100,000
Pension Plan	—0—	25,000	25,000
Profit-Sharing Plan	—0—	—0—	—0—
IRA	12,000	—0—	12,000
Life Insurance:			
Personal	50,000	—0—	50,000
Group	5,000	—0—	5,000
Personal Property:			
Automobile	—0—	5,000	5,000
Jewelry	—0—	5,000	5,000
Art	—0—	—0—	—0—

Fig. 13-5 (Page 2 of 2)

Furniture	—o—	5,000	5,000
Other Assets:			
COINS	2,000	—o—	2,000

Total Value of Estate $ 74,000 $ 247,000 $ 321,000

Fig. 13-6.

ESTIMATED ESTATE COSTS AND FEDERAL TAXES

Spouse #1

Total Value of Estate (from FIG. 13-5—

**total of separate and 50% of
jointly-owned property)** $ __321,000__

Deduct:

Debts $ ____-0-____

Funeral and last illness expenses[1]   ____5,000____

Income and other taxes due[2]   ____1,000____

Administration costs[3]   ____1,000____

   Total Deductions   (____7,000____)

   Gross Estate $ __314,000__

   Federal Estate Tax[4]   (____-0-____)

   Net Estate Available For Distribution to Beneficiaries $ __314,000__

---

1 An estimate will be required, $3,000-$5,000 should be sufficient unless a major illness is involved.
2 Any unpaid tax liabilities should be recorded.
3 For smaller or uncomplicated estates $500 to $1,000 should be sufficient, larger or more complex estates may require 5% to 10% of the estate value.
4 If the estate is over $600,000 a tax may be due. (A schedule is provided for this calculation.) For estates under $600,000, no federal estate tax will be due.

Fig. 13-7 (Page 1 of 2)

INVENTORY OF ASSETS

Spouse #1

Type of Property	Separately Owned	50% of Jointly Owned	Total
Cash:			
Checking Account	$ —0—	$ 10,000	$ 10,000
Savings Account	—0—	100,000	100,000
Securities:			
Stocks	—0—	50,000	50,000
Bonds	—0—	—0—	—0—
Mutual Funds	—0—	50,000	50,000
Receivables:			
Notes	—0—	—0—	—0—
Mortgages	—0—	—0—	—0—
Real Estate	50,000	—0—	50,000
Businesses	—0—	200,000	200,000
Residence	—0—	200,000	200,000
Pension Plan	100,000	—0—	100,000
Profit-Sharing Plan	50,000	—0—	50,000
IRA	10,000	—0—	10,000
Life Insurance:			
Personal	250,000	—0—	250,000
Group	50,000	—0—	50,000
Personal Property:			
Automobile	—0—	10,000	10,000
Jewelry	—0—	10,000	10,000
Art	—0—	—0—	—0—

Fig. 13-7 (Page 2 of 2)

Furniture	—0—	10,000	10,000
Other Assets:			

Total Value of Estate $ 510,000 $ 640,000 $ 1,150,000

Fig. 13-8

ESTIMATED ESTATE COSTS AND FEDERAL TAXES

Spouse #1

Total Value of Estate (from FIG. 13-7—

separately owned plus 50% of jointly owned property) $ *1,150,000*

Deduct:

Debts	$	*25,000*
Funeral and last illness expenses[1]		*5,000*
Income and other taxes due[2]		*5,000*
Administration costs[3]		*30,000*
Total Deductions		(*65,000*)
Gross Estate	$	*1,085,000*
Less: Federal Estate Tax[4]		(*NONE*)
Net Estate Available For Distribution to Beneficiaries	$	*1,085,000*

[1] An estimate will be required; $3,000-$5,000 should be sufficient unless a major illness is involved.
[2] Any unpaid tax liabilities should be recorded.
[3] For smaller or uncomplicated estates, $500 to $1,000 should be sufficient. Larger or more complex estates may require 5% to 10% of the estate value.
[4] If the estate is over $600,000 a tax may be due. (A schedule is provided for this calculation.) For estates under $600,000, no federal estate tax will be due.

Fig. 13-9

FEDERAL ESTATE TAX CALCULATION
(For Estates Over $600,000 In Value)

	Spouse #1	*Spouse #2*
Gross Estate[1]	_____	_____
Less: Marital Deduction[2]	(_____)	(_____)
Less: Contributions[3]	(_____)	(_____)
TAXABLE ESTATE	===========	===========
Federal Estate Tax[4]	_____	_____
Less: Unified Credit[5]	($192,800)	($192,800)
NET FEDERAL ESTATE TAX	===========	===========

[1] From Estimated Estate Costs and Taxes (FIG. 13-8).

[2] For married couples the taxable estate is reduced by the amount bequeathed to the surviving spouse. An assumption needs to be made between Spouse #1 and Spouse #2 as to who will die first. Generally it is assumed Spouse #1 will die first and the marital deduction will therefore only apply to the calculation for Spouse #1. If the entire estate is left to the surviving spouse, there will not be any federal estate tax.

[3] Any anticipated or directed charitable contributions are to be recorded.

[4] The federal estate-tax rate schedule should be consulted.

[5] The current credit is $192,800.

A man mortgaged his home for an automobile. Then he tried to
mortgage the automobile to get money to build a garage.
"How are you going to buy gas?" inquired the man of
whom the loan was asked.
"Well," replied the other slowly, "if I own a house, a car,
and a garage, I should think any dealer would be willing to trust
me for gas."

14

Major Purchases

Saving on Your Home and Car

EXCEPT FOR THE PURCHASE OF A HOME, MOST OF YOUR PURCHASES WILL NOT
help you reach your wealth accumulation goals. With knowledge, though, you'll
spend less money and have more remaining for investment purposes.

HOME PURCHASE

Your home will probably be the most expensive purchase you will make.
And the mortgage on the home will probably be your largest debt. In fact, it
has been said, if you want something that has a good chance of lasting forever,
sign a home mortgage!

How do you know how much debt you can handle comfortably? One rule
of thumb commonly used is that no more than 36% of your gross income should
go toward debt repayment (mortgage, car payments, charge cards, and any other
debt). Thus, if your gross monthly earnings are $2,500, no more than $900 should
go to debt repayment. If your gross earnings are $4,000 per month, a maximum
of $1,440 should go to debt repayment. This will give you a good idea of what
amount of debt you can handle and what price range of home you will be able
to afford. The monthly payment on a home is about one percent of the total mortgage, so a $100,000 mortgage will require a monthly payment of approximately
$1,000.

Once you have determined the amount of debt you can handle, you then need to determine the type of mortgage to obtain. The two most commonly available types of mortgages are *fixed-rate* mortgages and *adjustable-rate* mortgages.

Fixed-rate mortgages have a set rate of interest; it never varies during the term of the loan. You make the same monthly payment throughout the loan period.

Adjustable-rate mortgages, known as ARMs, have a variable interest rate. The monthly payment can vary as interest rates change. ARMs were first offered in California in 1970 and spread across the country by the early 1980s.

Initially, ARMs were limited almost exclusively to first-time home buyers who could not qualify for fixed-rate loans. However, they are now available to all home buyers. ARMs accounted for 68% of new mortgages at their peak of popularity in August 1984, but today, more than half of all new loans are fixed-rate.

ARMs have become more standardized, making it easier to compare one loan to another:

- Most ARMs are indexed to popular indexes (prime rate or major bank rate).

- There is usually a cap (limit) of two percentage points on yearly interest-rate increases. That is, no matter how high the index used may go, the mortgage rate can increase only 2% per year.

- There is usually an overall lifetime cap of 5%, up or down. So, no matter how high or low the index goes, your loan rate will not increase or decrease by more than 5% during the lifetime of the loan.

- There is a charge for loan processing, usually up to 2% of the overall loan.

In the first, second, and third years, ARMs are usually less costly than fixed-rate loans. This is true even if your rate increases after the first year. So if you plan to sell your home in two to three years, an ARM will save interest expense. But if you plan to hold your home seven to ten years, the savings is generally lost, and a fixed rate is less costly.

To illustrate, let's assume that you want a $100,000, 30-year loan and have a choice of a 12.5% fixed-rate mortgage or an ARM that starts out at 10.4%. If the home were sold in the third year, there would be a savings of about $2,000 with the ARM, even though the ARM increases to 12.4% in the second year. If the home were held 10 years, however, the ARM would cost an additional

$15,000 in interest expense, assuming an average rate of 14%. An average rate of 16% would cost $26,000 more than the fixed-rate mortgage at 12.5%.

You also have a choice of a 30-year or a 15-year loan. Though the monthly payments on a 15-year loan will be higher, the overall savings on interest expense will be significant. With a $100,000, 12.5% fixed-rate mortgage, a 30-year loan would cost $162,000 more in interest than a 15-year loan. The difference in the monthly payment would be $165. So, if you can handle the additional cost each month, a 15-year loan would be the wiser choice.

EXISTING MORTGAGE

If you have an existing 30-year mortgage, check with your lender to see if you can increase your mortgage payment by $50, $100, or more per month, with the additional payment applied to principal. If this is allowed you could save a significant amount of money in interest expense. By just paying $50 additional against the principal in the first month of a 30-year mortgage, you would save over $2,000 in interest expense over the remaining life of that loan. By continuing to do so each month, the resulting savings would be tens of thousands of dollars over the life of the mortgage.

SELLING A HOME

Two special tax benefits are available if you sell your home. The first is available to all individuals. The second is available only to those 55 years of age or older.

Deferral of Gain

If you sell your principal residence, and within two years before or after that date, purchase a new residence, you must defer any gain recognized if the adjusted purchase price of the new residence exceeds the adjusted selling price of the old residence. The new residence must be used as the principal residence.

For example, a home purchased in 1978 for $80,000 is sold in January 1988 for $150,000. The $70,000 gain will not be recognized if the new residence costs at least $150,000. If the new residence costs less, for example, $140,000, there would be a taxable gain, in this case, $10,000.

A gain that is not currently recognized is merely postponed. That is, the cost of the new home is reduced, for tax purposes, by the gain not recognized. In the above example, there was a $70,000 gain not taxed and thus the $150,000 cost of the new home will have a tax basis of $80,000. If that home is later sold and a new home is not purchased, the gain would then be taxed.

When determining your gain on the sale of a residence, whether taxed currently or deferred, the cost of improvements to the house being sold (room additions, remodeling, landscaping, wallpaper, appliances and fixtures, carpeting, etc.) need to be added to the house's original cost. And don't forget to add the closing costs incurred when the house was first purchased (commissions, attorney fees, escrow fees, title insurance, appraisals, etc.). All of these expenses, plus the original purchase price, will determine the adjusted tax basis of the house sold.

The price that you sell the old house for needs to be adjusted as well. Deduct your selling expenses (broker's commission, title fees, attorney fees, escrow fees, transfer taxes, etc.) from the price you received for the old house. This balance is called the *amount realized*. Then deduct any expenses you incurred in fixing up the property for sale (painting, repairing, etc.) from the amount realized. This balance is the *adjusted selling price*.

The purchase price of your new home is also adjusted. It is increased by the closing costs you paid (title fees, attorney fees, appraisals, escrow fees, etc.).

All of the adjustments discussed above will determine the tax deferral and what, if anything, is taxable currently. FIGURE 14-1 can be used to determine the tax basis and taxability of a sale of your residence.

In FIG. 14-2 the adjusted purchase price of a new residence ($152,000) exceeds the adjusted sales price ($139,000) by $13,000; therefore, the entire $49,000 gain on the sale of the old home is deferred. The adjusted purchase price of the new home is reduced by this postponed gain of $49,000 and for tax purposes now has a cost basis of $103,000. If this house is subsequently sold for $200,000 and a new home is not purchased, a taxable gain of $97,000 ($200,000 less $103,000 tax basis) would result.

If in FIG. 14-2 the newly purchased home had an adjusted purchase price of $135,000, the results would be as follows:

A. Adjusted Purchase Price of New Home $ 135,000
B. Less: Adjusted Selling Price of Old Home   (139,000)
C. Difference   (4,000)

As the example indicates, the adjusted purchase price of the new home is less than the adjusted selling price of the old home; therefore, the difference of $4,000 will be subject to tax currently. The remaining gain of $45,000 ($49,000 total gain less $4,000 currently taxed) will be deferred.

These rules are mandatory. If line A is greater than line B, you *must* postpone the gain.

Once-in-a-Lifetime Exclusion of Gain

Persons who have attained age 55 prior to the date of sale of their principal residence may elect to exclude up to $125,000 of the gain realized on the sale. For married couples who file separate returns, the maximum exclusion is $62,500 on each separate return.

To qualify for this exclusion, you must also have owned and used the residence as the principal residence for a total of at least three years during the five-year period ending on the date of sale. (A residence, for this purpose, includes a condominium or the stock of a shareholder-tenant in a cooperative housing corporation.) For married couples who hold their residence as joint tenants, tenants by the entirety, or community property and file a joint return for the year of the sale, if one spouse meets the age, ownership, and use requirements, then both spouses qualify.

This exclusion is available to a person only once in a lifetime, and married couples are entitled to only one election per couple. In addition, if spouses make an election during marriage and they subsequently divorce, no further election is available to either of them or to their future spouses should they remarry. On the other hand, if two unmarried people who have each made an independent election subsequently remarry, there is no recapture of the tax on the gains previously excluded.

For ease of discussion, the tax laws discussed in this section have been generalized. Consult IRS Publications #523 and #530 for complete details on the tax consequences of selling a home.

AUTOMOBILES

When you are in the market for a new car, the choice of make, model, style, color, and options is further complicated by the choice of whether to purchase or lease the car.

Generally, buying a car is less expensive than leasing one, especially if it is an all-cash purchase. A leasing company may very well mark up a 12% auto loan to 20% or 22%. Over the life of a lease, you will pay significantly more than you will for a bank loan. But a lease can be a good tool to use if you tend to change automobiles frequently or you do not have the cash for a down payment on an auto loan (though, for the more expensive cars, many banks are reducing or eliminating the down payment).

With the changes made by the Tax Reform Act, leasing may have become more attractive. There are three changes that tend to favor the leasing of an automobile:

- Sales Tax—The sales tax you pay on a new car is no longer deductible.

- Interest Deductions—The deduction for personal interest, which includes auto loans, is being phased out. Only 40% of the interest is deductible in 1988, 20% in 1989, 10% in 1990, and none thereafter.

- Tax Rates—Tax rates have been reduced, at least for the time being, to a top rate of 33%. That means that any interest deduction remaining under the phaseout period may be less valuable to you.

The net effect of all of these changes is that the tax benefits of buying a car have been sharply reduced.

Leasing has been affected by the Tax Reform Act as well:

- Investment Credit—The investment credit on equipment purchases, including automobiles, has been repealed. A leasing company has thus lost a significant way of reducing its own tax bill.

- Depreciation Deductions—The time it takes to write-off a car for tax purposes has been stretched out from three years to five years. This slows down the leasing company's cost recovery.

The net effect of these two changes will most probably cause the leasing company to pass along the lost tax benefits in the form of higher leasing rates.

There is a misconception among many individuals that if a car is used for business it must be leased in order to obtain any tax deductions. This is not true. When you lease a car, the lease payments are the tax deduction. When you purchase a car, the tax deduction is based on the depreciation of the car over a five-year period. There are numerous regulations regarding the personal use of a business car, luxury cars, and recordkeeping. These details are beyond the scope of this book. Suffice it to say that tax deductions are available whether a business car is leased or purchased.

When you are faced with the choice of buying or leasing a car, also consider these non-tax aspects:

- No down payment is normally required when you lease a car. If cash is tight, leasing becomes more attractive.

- When your lease term is up, you have to pay the leasing company for the car if you want to keep it. At that point the choice becomes: (1) paying for a used car or (2) losing the benefit of your past lease payments and starting all over again.

- Most leasing companies impose a penalty fee (5 to 10 cents per mile) if a car is driven more than a certain number of miles. The normal mileage is 15,000 miles per year. If the car is turned in (instead of being purchased) at the end of the lease term with a mileage reading in excess of the normal mileage stated in the contract, the penalty fee will be imposed. For example, if you turn in a car with 60,000 miles at the end of a three-year lease, the additional 15,000 miles above the normal three-year mileage of 45,000 miles could be subject to a penalty of $750 to $1500.

There is no clear-cut advantage to either leasing or buying. Much depends on your personal and tax circumstances. You need to review the pros and cons of the two choices and determine which method will serve your needs best.

If you decide to buy, and need to obtain an auto loan, shop around. Rates can vary significantly. Major automobile companies' credit divisions, such as GMAC, typically charge more than local banks, except when those companies advertise promotional rates to help sell their cars. It is also possible that, even if the dealer has a connection with a local bank, the rates he quotes will be somewhat higher than you might obtain if you shop around yourself. Credit unions usually offer the lowest auto loan rates.

Many companies now make auto loans for up to five years, depending on the price of the automobile. The more expensive the automobile, the longer the terms. There are even companies and banks that are assuming an equity or salvage value after the term of the loan. They may assume that the $20,000 car you are currently purchasing will have a value of $15,000 in three years, so you will pay off only a $5,000 loan over three years as opposed to a $20,000 loan. At the termination of the loan, either the bank will take back the automobile, or you will pay off the remaining amount. This type of loan is offered on expensive luxury cars because the risk to the bank is reduced by the cars' minimal depreciation. Monthly payments on a Mercedes or a Porsche, for example, might be the same as you would pay for a Chevrolet or Ford.

What about the other costs of using an automobile? For business use of automobiles, the IRS allows either a standard per-mile deduction or actual expenses. A recent study by the Hertz Corporation indicated that the actual cost per mile averages about 60 cents while the IRS only allows 24 cents. So don't be lazy. Retain all of your gas and oil receipts, repair receipts, insurance premium stubs, license fee receipts, etc., and at the end of each year, calculate how much it actually cost you to run the automobile. If you use the car 80% for business, you will receive 80% of that amount as a deduction, plus depreciation on the automobile. This should increase your deduction significantly over the standard mileage rate.

Choosing which car to buy has become a very complicated, exhausting, and many times, frustrating experience. Just as important, however, are the method of purchase—buying vs. leasing—and the terms of that purchase. Shop around, ask questions, and make sure you thoroughly understand not only what you are buying, but what the costs are as well.

Fig. 14-1 (Page 1 of 2)

Adjusted Cost Basis of Old Home

Original Purchase Price of Old Home $ _____
Original Closing Costs of Old Home
   Attorney Fees $ _____
   Escrow Fees   _____
   Title Insurance   _____
   Appraisal Fees   _____
   Transfer Fees   _____
     Original Closing Costs of Old Home
      Cost Basis of Old Home $ _____
Improvements to Old Home:
   Landscaping $ _____
   Carpeting   _____
   Room Additions   _____
   Appliances   _____
   New Roof   _____
   New Water Heater   _____
    Total Improvements to Old Home   _____
ADJUSTED COST BASIS OF OLD HOME $ _____

Gain on Sale of Old Home

Selling Price of Old Home $ _____
Less: Selling Expenses
   Broker's Commissions   ($ _____)
   Title Insurance   (_____)
   Transfer Fees   (_____)
   Appraisals   (_____)
   Attorney Fees   (_____)
   Escrow Fees   (_____)
    Total Selling Expenses   (_____)
    Amount Realized $ _____
Less: Fixing-Up Expenses
   Painting   ($ _____)
   Repairs   (_____)
   Cement Work   (_____)
    Total Fixing-Up Expenses   (_____)

Fig. 14-1 (Page 2 of 2)

ADJUSTED SELLING PRICE OF OLD HOME   _____
LESS: ADJUSTED COST BASIS OF OLD HOME   (_____)
GAIN (OR LOSS[1]) ON SALE OF OLD HOME   _____

Adjusted Purchase Price of New Home

Purchase Price of New Home $ _____
Closing Costs of New Home:
   Broker Commissions   _____
   Attorney Fees   _____
   Escrow   _____
   Title Policy   _____
   Transfer Fees   _____
ADJUSTED PURCHASE PRICE OF NEW HOME $ _____

A. Adjusted Purchase Price of New Home $ _____
B. Adjusted Selling Price of Old Home $ _____
C. Difference $ _____

If A is greater than B, you must defer the Gain on Sale of Old Home, calculated earlier.
If A is less than or equal to B, you will be taxed currently on the gain or on the amount
on line C, whichever is less.

Tax Basis of New Home After Deferral of Gain

Adjusted Purchase Price of New Home $ _____
Less: Gain not currently taxed   ($ _____)
TAX BASIS OF NEW HOME $ _____

1 There is no recognition, for tax purposes, of a loss on the sale of a principal residence. The loss is completely ignored and the
basis of a residence purchased after the loss is incurred is not adjusted.

Fig. 14-2 (Page 1 of 2)

Adjusted Cost Basis of Old Home

Original Purchase Price of Old Home		$ 80,000
Original Closing Costs of Old Home		
Attorney Fees	$ 500	
Escrow Fees	300	
Title Insurance	200	
Appraisal Fees	500	
Transfer Fees	500	
Original Closing Costs of Old Home		2,000
Cost Basis of Old Home		$ 82,000
Improvements to Old Home:		
Landscaping	$ 5,000	
Carpeting	2,000	
Room Additions	–0–	
Appliances	500	
New Roof	–0–	
New Water Heater	500	
Total Improvements to Old Home		8,000
ADJUSTED COST BASIS OF OLD HOME		$ 90,000

Gain on Sale of Old Home

Selling Price of Old Home		$ 150,000
Less: Selling Expenses		
Broker's Commissions	($ 6,500)	
Title Insurance	(500)	
Transfer Fees	(500)	
Appraisals	(500)	
Attorney Fees	(500)	
Escrow Fees	(500)	
Total Selling Expenses		(9,000)
Amount Realized		$ 141,000
Less: Fixing-Up Expenses		
Painting	($ 1,000)	
Repairs	(500)	
Cement Work	(500)	
Total Fixing-Up Expenses		(2,000)

Fig. 14-2 (Page 2 of 2)

ADJUSTED SELLING PRICE OF OLD HOME $\qquad$ *139,000*
LESS: ADJUSTED COST BASIS OF OLD HOME (*90,000*)
GAIN (OR LOSS[1]) ON SALE OF OLD HOME $\qquad$ *49,000*

Adjusted Purchase Price of New Home

Purchase Price of New Home $ *150,000*
Closing Costs of New Home:
   Broker Commissions   *—o—*
   Attorney Fees   *500*
   Escrow   *500*
   Title Policy   *500*
   Transfer Fees   *500*
ADJUSTED PURCHASE PRICE OF NEW HOME $ *152,000*

A. Adjusted Purchase Price of New Home $ *152,000*
B. Adjusted Selling Price of Old Home $ *139,000*
C. Difference $ *13,000*

If A is greater than B, you must defer the Gain on Sale of Old Home, calculated earlier.
If A is less than or equal to B, you will be taxed currently on the gain or on the amount
on line C, whichever is less.

Tax Basis of New Home After Deferral of Gain

Adjusted Purchase Price of New Home $ *152,000*
Less: Gain not currently taxed   (*49,000*)
TAX BASIS OF NEW HOME $ *103,000*

1 There is no recognition, for tax purposes, of a loss on the sale of a principal residence. The loss is completely ignored and the
  basis of a residence purchased after the loss is incurred is not adjusted.

The man who saves money nowadays isn't a miser; he's a wizard.

15

The 10% Solution

NOW THAT YOU HAVE READ THE BOOK AND COMPLETED THE WORKSHEETS YOU can see that there is no longer a "mystery" to financial planning and increasing your wealth. You can do it; you *are* doing it!

Always put aside *10% Off the Top*. Let there be no exceptions. Consider it like any other monthly bill—rent, telephone, utilities. You must pay the rent, and you must pay yourself the 10%.

Keep complete and accurate records. Review the worksheets you prepared in Chapter 2 (you have prepared them, haven't you?) and update them periodically, at least once a year.

Stick to your budget. I know it's difficult, but it's worth the effort. If you find that you can't meet certain budgeted items, review the other expenses to see if any can be reduced to accommodate the increases. Compare your budget to your actual expenses on a monthly basis. If you had a bad month and went over budget, try to make up for it the following month.

Review your insurance coverage on at least an annual basis. If your circumstances change and you need more or less coverage, don't hesitate to contact your agent or insurance company. If your employer, for example, increases your life insurance coverage, you may want to reduce your other life insurance coverage accordingly.

If you have children, continue to monitor your educational funding plan. Reread Chapter 6 periodically. Contact the high school and colleges for their guidance as your children approach college age. Student loan programs and the like are continually changing.

Don't ignore preparations for your retirement. Continue to monitor the retirement programs you are involved in. Know your rights and the benefits available. Read the material provided by the various plans, and ask questions if you don't understand something. And don't forget to request a printout of your social security account.

Taxes have become increasingly complicated over the past few years. Don't shy away from your own tax planning. Try to understand the basis of your own income tax situation. No one can be as familiar with your finances as you. Review Chapter 11 and the Appendices. Each year read the instruction booklet mailed to you by the IRS; it has good information that will apply to you.

As your wealth increases, don't be afraid to shop around for your investments. Rates—and risk—do vary. Talk to professionals; they will be glad to answer your questions. Always comparison shop; buying a certificate of deposit should be no different from buying a TV.

You do have your will prepared and signed, don't you? If you don't, please do it *now*! As your circumstances change you may need to change provisions, beneficiaries, etc. Review your estate plan on an annual basis.

When you buy or sell your residence, or when you buy or lease an automobile, be aware of the various rules and options available to you. Be a smart consumer. Review Chapter 14 before and during the negotiations. Don't be afraid to ask questions, and don't accept an answer unless you understand it completely.

The various steps and tools you have learned and acquired from this book are not difficult to follow. And by following them you can assure yourself of a healthy financial future. Saving *10% Off the Top* has been discussed in detail. Hopefully, you are convinced of its merits and have made it a habit. If you're not convinced yet, the following examples should bring you around.

- A 25 year old, earning a net income of $24,000 a year or $2,000 a month, saves $200 each month (10% of $2,000). If he or she receives 3% salary increases each year and earns interest on savings at an average of 7% per year, at the age of 65 this individual will have accumulated $727,300.

- A 45 year old, earning a net income of $30,000 a year or $2,500 a month, saves $250 each month. If this individual receives 3% annual salary increases and a savings return of 7%, at age 65 he or she will have accumulated $160,200.

Can't save 10%? If the individuals in the above examples save only 5% ($100/month in the first case, $125/month in the second), they will still accumulate $363,700 and $80,100, respectively, by age 65.

Still not convinced? Let's assume that they only save 1% (that's only $20/month in the first case, $25/month in the second). At age 65 they would still have saved $72,700 and $16,000, respectively.

It adds up, doesn't it? The monthly savings may not appear to be all that much, but over the years, by continually following the plan, you can save big bucks *painlessly*.

What are you waiting for? It doesn't matter what age you are. Start saving *10% Off the Top. Make it a habit*!

People think taxation is a terribly mundane subject. But what makes it fascinating is that taxation, in reality, is life. If you know the position a person takes on taxes, you can tell their whole philosophy. The tax code, once you get to know it, embodies all the essence of life: greed, politics, power, goodness, charity. Everything's in there. That's why it's so hard to get a simplified tax code. Life just isn't simple.—*Former IRS Commissioner Sheldon Cohen*

Appendix A

Taxable and Nontaxable Income

Fig. A-1 (Page 1 of 3)

TAXABLE INCOME

Agreement not to compete, payments received for

Alimony, support, and separate maintenance payments, receipts of

Annuities (in excess of cost)

Annuities, premium for prepayment discount

Antitrust action, punitive damages recovered

Armed Forces pay (except "combat zone" or "missing" status pay)

Awards (unless transferred by recipient)

Back pay

Bargain purchases from employer to extent discount exceeds gross profit percentage

Beauty contest winners, receipt of scholarships and amounts for personal appearances

Bonds, issue of premiums on

Bonuses

Buried treasure

Business interruption insurance proceeds—based on income experience

Business profits

Checks, uncashed by payee, for previously deducted items

Christmas bonuses from employer, based on percentage of salary, but not the value of hams, turkeys, etc., given for goodwill

Clergy, fees and contributions received unless overtly of religious order

Commissions

Compensation, property received, value of

Contract cancellation, payments received for

Damages—loss of anticipatory benefits (business)

Death benefits—where employee contributed nothing to employer's plan and rights were nonforfeitable

Debts, cancellation of, generally

Discharge of indebtedness

Dividends

Dividends—stock distributed in lieu of money

Drawing account, excess cancelled by employer

Embezzlement proceeds

Employment contract, amounts received by employee for cancellation

Evangelist, contributions received

Fig. A-1 (Page 2 of 3)

Farm income
Farmers, government payments to offset operating losses or lack of profits
Financial counseling fees, employer-paid
Future services, prepayment of
Gains—condemnation of nonresidential property except where award is used for replacement
Gains—discount on later sale or redemption bonds purchased with excess number of interest coupons detached
Gains—obligations purchased or satisfied for less than face value
Gains—partner's sale of asset to partnership
Gains—sales of city and state bonds, U.S. securities, depreciable property, goodwill, patents and copyrights, property, stock in foreign corporations, stock of foreign investment company
Gains—swap-fund transfers
Gambling winnings
Government employees, additional compensation as inducement to accept foreign service employment
Health resort expenses, employer-paid
Hedging transactions, commodity futures transactions
Illegal transactions, gains from—gambling, betting, lotteries, illegal business, embezzlement, protection money, etc.
Illness, employee's compensation during, except to extent not qualifying as sick pay
Income tax refunds, state—to extent of tax benefit
Insider's profits
Insurance proceeds—use of occupancy, actual loss of net profits
Interest on bank deposits or accounts, claim awarded by judgment, condemnation awards, deferred legacies, federal obligations, insurance contracts, refund of federal taxes, short-term paper
Jury fees
Layoff pay benefits—benefit plan, company-financed; supplemental unemployment
Lease cancellation, payments received for
Libel or slander of personal reputation, exemplary damages
Life insurance dividends, veteran's converted, interest on
Living quarters and meals, unless furnished for employer's convenience
Losses, previously deducted, reimbursement for, or expense items
Military personnel, per diem pay
Military service, employer payments to employees

Mortgage indebtedness, repayment at a discount to the extent of the discount
Moving expenses, employer reimbursement
National Labor Relations Board, back pay award
Notary public fees
Obligations, federal interest on
Partnership, distributive share of taxable income
Patents, sale to controlled foreign corporation
Pensions—distributions attributable to employer contributions
Professional fee
Purchases, employee discounts
Receiver's fees
Reconditioning expenses, employer-paid
Relocation assistance benefits, paid by landlords to tenants under a municipal
    ordinance
Rents
Retirement pay attributable to employee's contributions other than veterans dis-
    ability retirement pay
Royalties
Salaries
Security deposits, when retained by lessor
Stock options—other than qualified options
Support payment, for former spouse
Taxes—employee's, employer-paid
Taxes—lessee paid (income to lessor)
Tenancy, surrender of, payments for
Tips
Tuition, employer-paid, unless under qualified plans
Unemployment benefit plans, supplemental payments
Unemployment benefits
U.S. savings bonds, earned increase during year, if cash-method taxpayer
    elects
Use and occupancy insurance proceeds, income experience
Wages

Fig. A-2 (Page 1 of 2)

NONTAXABLE ITEMS

Accident and health insurance premiums, employer-paid

Accident and health plan proceeds (under insurance purchased by taxpayer or under employee-supported plans) where premiums did not give taxpayer a previous medical expense deduction

Allowances received by dependents of deceased members of the armed forces

Athletic facilities on employer's premises, value of use

Bad debts, prior taxes and interest on taxes, recovery of no tax benefit in prior year

Bequests and devises

Bonds, state, city, etc., interest on

Business interruption insurance proceeds—based on per diem idleness

Business subsidies for construction or contributions to capital

Capital contributions to corporation

Car pool receipts by car owner for transportation of fellow employees

Car used for business purposes by full-time car salesperson, value of use

Child or dependent care plan benefits, employer-subsidized

Child support payments

"Combat zone" pay, military

Damages—breach of promise to marry, personal injuries or sickness, slander or libel of personal reputation

Death benefits—up to $5,000, employer-paid

Dependent care assistance program payments up to $5,000

Disability payments, other than for loss of wages, all taxpayers, including veterans

Disability pensions, Veterans Administration

Dividends—unmatured life insurance policies

Educational assistance, employer-provided, nondiscriminatory plan up to $5,250

Employee discount, qualified

Endowment policies, proceeds, until cost recovered

Fellowship and scholarship grants, for degree candidates

Foreign earned income, limited

Foster parents, reimbursements for care of a qualified foster child

Fringe benefits, if no additional cost service, qualified employee discount, working condition fringe, de minimis fringe

Gain on sale of personal residence—replacement residence

Gain on sale of personal residence—up to $125,000 taxpayer age 55 and over

Fig. A-2 (Page 2 of 2)

Gifts

Health insurance proceeds, not attributable to premiums that gave medical expense deduction in prior years

Income tax refunds—federal

Inheritances

Involuntary conversions, gain from, if reinvested

Juror's mileage allowance

Legal services plan, payments received for and value of benefits received

Lessee's improvements, value of to lessor upon termination of lease

Life insurance, group-term premiums, paid by employer, to extent of employer's cost of $50,000 or less of insurance

Life insurance proceeds, paid on death of the insured

Living expenses, damaged home being repaired

Lodging, cost of, furnished by employer for its convenience

Medical care payments, employer-financed accident and health plan

Mustering-out pay

National Service Life Insurance dividends

Parsonage, rental value of, furnished to a minister or rabbi as part of compensation; rental allowances if used to rent or provide a home

Peace Corps volunteers, basic living and travel allowances

Political campaign contributions, with exceptions

Railroad Retirement Act benefits, partial exclusion

Scholarships and fellowship grants, for degree candidates

Sickness and injury benefits—employer's plan, subject to limitations

Sickness and injury benefits—workers' compensation equivalent

Social Security old age, disability, and survivor's benefits, partial exclusion

State contracts, profits on, essential governmental function

Stock options—qualified

Strike benefits, union and non-union employees in need

Supper money, employer-paid, for employer's benefit

Surviving spouse, decedent's salary continued, limited

Taxes—refunds of, not previously deducted or deducted without tax benefit

Treaty—exempt income

Veterans Administration payments

Veteran's benefits

Veteran's bonuses, state

War risk insurance proceeds paid on maturity of policy

Worker's compensation acts, payments under

I'm proud to be paying taxes in the United States. The only thing is—I could be just as proud for half the money.—*Arthur Godfrey*

Appendix B

Deductible and Nondeductible Expenses

Fig. B-1 (Page 1 of 4)

MISCELLANEOUS DEDUCTIONS

Accountant's fees, connected with production of income

Administration expenses of estate

Alimony payments

Amortization of premium on taxable bonds (optional)

Attorney's fees, business protection of beneficiary's trust interests; collection fees; collection of social security disability payments

Bad debts

Baseball player's uniforms

Baseball team equipment for business publicity

Bookmaker's rents, wages, etc.

Business expenses

Business gifts of $25 or less per donee per taxable year

Business start-up costs

Carrying charges deductible as interest where installment sales contract states carrying charge separately

Casualty loss to property in excess of $100 (total losses allowed if in excess of 10% of adjusted gross income)

Charitable contributions by individuals and corporations

Club dues and house bills (business)

Commissions on sale of real estate and securities (dealer only; other taxpayers deduct from selling price)

Compensation paid

Condominium, interest and taxes

Contributions by employer to state unemployment insurance and state disability funds

Contributions by employer under union-government-negotiated plans to a welfare trust for benefit of employees

Contributions by employers to employer-financed accident and health plans for benefit of employees

Contributions by members to labor union

Contributions paid by employer to employee's trust or annuity plan

Contributions paid (within certain limits) during year to charitable, etc., organizations

Cooperative housing corporation, taxes or interest paid to

Corporate organizational expenditures (if election is made to amortize)

Custodian fees

Depreciation—business property, property held for production of income, newspaper subscription list

Disbarment proceedings, attorney's fees and expenses in defending

Dividends, amounts paid by dealer in securities in place of dividends on short sales

Dues, paid to professional societies or business associations

Education expense which maintains or improves skills or meets the express requirements of employer, law, or regulations for retention of salary, status, or employment

Educational assistance program payments

Efficiency engineer's fee paid to reduce cost of business operations

Employee's expenses—automobile expenses; entertaining customers; meals and lodging while away from home including tips, telephone and telegraph expenses, baggage charges, public stenographer's fees; moving expenses incident to commencing work at a new location; transportation expenses including railroad, airplane, boat, local bus, taxi, streetcar, etc., fares and tips (other than cost of commuting to and from work)

Employees, payments to, for injuries not compensated by insurance; disability benefits

Employment, fees for obtaining

Entertaining customers or employees

Excess deductions on termination of estate or trust

Expenses incurred in earning taxable income

Finance charges

Firefighter's rubber coat, helmet, boots, etc.

Franchise or license, cost of acquiring from state or governmental authorities (deductible ratably over life of license)

Gifts (business) up to $25 per donee per year

Income tax liability, cost of determining

Income tax returns, cost of preparing (business and nonbusiness)

Infringement litigation in course of business

Injuries to employees, payments for, not compensated by insurance

Interest (subject to limitations) except on indebtedness incurred or continued to purchase or carry tax-exempt securities or single-premium life insurance, endowment, or annuity contracts, and except on loan to cover payment of substantial number of premiums on a life insurance or annuity policy

Investor's expenses (except incurred in earning tax-exempt interest)

Labor union dues

Fig. B-1 (Page 3 of 4)

Leased computer equipment expenses

Legal fees for contesting estate, gift, property, and other taxes, whether state or federal

Lobbying expenses (limited)

Lucky number contest, cost of prizes

Mortgage prepayment penalty

Moving expenses to new place of employment

Moving machinery to new plant

Musician's dress clothes, used exclusively in business, including maintenance expenses

Net operating losses carried back or over

Nontrade or nonbusiness expenses incurred in preserving income-producing property

Nurse's uniform, for private duty or in contagious hospital

Operating loss in prior or subsequent year

Organization expenses of corporation (amortizable over not less than 60 months)

Partner's fixed or guaranteed payments for services or for use of capital

Passport fee, business trip

Penalty, prepayment of mortgage deductible as interest

Points on home mortgage (if customarily required in geographic area in which indebtedness is incurred) excluding refinance points

Police officer's uniform and cost of cleaning

Premiums paid on "professional overhead expense disability policy"

Professional journals (but not by an employee)

Reconditioning and health-restoring expenses of employees paid by employers

Reimbursed expenses in connection with employment (if included in income)

Rent, business property

Repairs to business property

Research and experimental expenditures connected with a trade or business if amortized

Return, federal or state income tax, gift tax, etc., cost of having prepared (including an investor)

Safe-deposit boxes, rental for protection of income-producing property

Salaries, business

Salesperson's expenses—automobile expenses, entertaining customers, membership dues (in appropriate circumstances) in business or social clubs, presents for customers, travel expenses

Self-employed person's health insurance
Start-up costs for business
Surgeon's uniform
Tax determination and litigation expenses where connected with taxpayer's
    business
Tax refresher course, lawyer's
Tax return, cost of preparing
Theft
Tools, life of one year or less
Traveling expenses, business trips; for example:
    Baseball players (including meals and lodging) while away from "home club"
        town; also other business expenses at "home club" town if tax "home"
        in a different city
    Clergymen, church conventions
    Commercial fishing boat crewmembers, for travel, meals and lodging away
        from home port
    Congressmen, up to $3,000 of living expenses
    Employee, away from home
    Government employees, expenses up to maximum per diem allowances
    Lawyer—on professional business, bar association meetings
    Merchants
    Physician, medical conventions
    Professional golfers
    Railroad employee's meals and lodging while away from "home terminal"
    Salesperson, traveling away from home (see also salesperson's expenses
        above)
    Teachers, scientific meetings and conventions
    Truck drivers (long line), meals and lodging while away from "home terminal"
Traveling expenses from principal place to minor place of business
Truck tires, with life of less than a year
Uncollectible notes
Uniforms, cost and cleaning, if not adaptable for general wear
Union dues
Work shoes, metal-tipped for protection of worker
Worthless securities

Fig. B-2

CAPITAL EXPENDITURES
(ADDED TO COST OF ITEM)
Not Deductible at the Time that the Cost Is Incurred

Admission to bar, traveling expense in securing

Advances to insolvent corporation

Architect's fees

Attorney's fees—in acquiring property; reducing local benefit assessment

Automobile finance charges (except amount determined to be interest)

Bar examination fees

Bondholder's committee expense assessments

Building replacements

Burglar alarm system, cost of installing

Commissions on purchase or sale of real estate or securities (except selling commissions of dealers)

Construction period interest and taxes (except for low-income housing, property not used in a trade or business or in an activity conducted for profit; and residential real property of a corporation other than an S corporation, personal holding company, or foreign personal holding company)

Copyright costs

Corporate organization expenses unless election to amortize

Defending title to property

Development expenses, as in the case of a patent, unless election to deduct currently or amortize

Fees in obtaining professional licenses

Insurance premiums during building operations at taxpayer's election

Interest and carrying charges related to a commodity straddle position

Investigating prospective business

Legal expenses paid to recover property

New buildings, machinery, equipment, fixtures

Organization expenditures, unless election to amortize

Partnership organization expenses, unless election to amortize

Patents, cost of procuring (except through deduction of research and development expenses)

Permanent improvements

Professional books of attorney

Sprinkler system, installation of, in apartment / hotel

Title costs (perfecting or defending title to property)

Trademark, cost of renewing

Fig. B-3 (Page 1 of 3)

DEDUCTIBLE MEDICAL EXPENSES

Abortion, legal
Acupuncture
Adoption—medical costs of adopted child
Air conditioner—allergy relief
Alcoholism, treatment of
Ambulance hire
Attendants to accompany blind student
Blindness—special educational aids to mitigate condition
Braille books and magazines—excess cost of regular editions
Capital expenditure—primary purpose: medical care
Car equipped to accommodate wheelchair passengers
Car handicap controls
Chiropractors
Christian Science treatment
Clarinet and lessons—alleviation of severe tooth malocclusion
Computer data bank—storage and retrieval of medical records
Contact lenses
Contraceptives, prescription
Cosmetic surgery
Crutches
Dental fees
Diagnostic fees
Diapers, disposable—used due to severe neurological disease
Doctors
Domestic aid—type that would be rendered by nurse
Drug addiction, recovery from
Drug prescription
Electrolysis
Elevator—alleviation of cardiac condition
Eye examinations and glasses
Face lift
Fluoride device
Glasses
Guide animals, cost and maintenance of

Fig. B-3 (Page 2 of 3)

Hair transplants, surgical
Halfway house—adjustment to community following stay in mental hospital
Health insurance for self-employed (25% of costs)
Health Maintenance Organization (HMO)
Hearing aids—notetaker for student; telephone, specially equipped; television, closed-caption decoder; visual alert system
Hospital care, in-patient
Hospital services
Insulin
Insurance, Medicare A coverage—premiums for medical
Iron lung
Laboratory fees
Laetrile, legal use
Lead paint removal
Legal expenses—authorization of treatment for mental illness
Lifetime medical care, prepaid
Limbs, artificial
Lip-reading expenses for deaf
Lodging—limited to $50 per night
Mattress prescribed for alleviation of arthritis
Notetaker for deaf student
Nurse's fee—including board if paid by taxpayer
Nursing home—medical reasons
Obstetrical expenses
Operation, legal
Orthodontia
Orthopedic shoes, excess cost of
Osteopaths
Oxygen equipment for breathing difficulty
Patterning exercises for handicapped child
Plumbing—special fixtures for handicapped
Psychiatric care
Psychologist
Psychotherapists
Reclining chair for cardiac patient
Remedial reading
Retirement home, life care
Sanitarium rest home, cost of—medical, educational, or rehabilitative reasons

Fig. B-3 (Page 3 of 3)

Schools, special—relief of handicapped
Sexual dysfunction, hospitalization for
Sterilization operation
Swimming pool for treatment of polio
Taxicab to doctor's office
Teeth, artificial
Telephone, specially equipped—for the deaf
Television—closed-caption decoder
Transplant, donor's cost of
Transportation—cost incurred essentially and primarily for medical care
Vasectomy, legal
Visual alert system for hearing-impaired
Wheelchair
Wigs needed after medical treatment
X-rays

Fig. B-3A

NONDEDUCTIBLE MEDICAL EXPENSES

Anticipated medical expenses
Babysitting
Capital expenditures—permanent improvement to property
Car, depreciation
Car insurance—medical coverage
Chauffeur, salary of
Clothing
Crime victims—compensated medical expenses
Dancing lessons
Deprogramming services
Diaper service
Dust elimination system
Ear piercing
Fallout shelter—prevention of disease
Funeral expenses
Furnace
Gravestone
Health club dues
Hygienic supplies
Legal expenses for divorce upon medical advice
Marriage counseling
Maternity clothes
Residence, loss on sale of—move medically recommended
Self-help, medical
Spiritual guidance
Stop-smoking program
Tattoos
Toilet articles
Trips for general health improvement
Vacations, health-restorative
Vacuum cleaner for alleviation of dust allergy
Weight loss programs, prescribed

Fig. B-3B.

DEDUCTIBLE INVESTOR EXPENSES

Accountant's fees
Collection services
Commodity tax straddle losses (to the extent they exceed unrealized gains)
Custodian's fees
Dividends paid on stock borrowed to cover short sales
Investment counsel fee
Legal fee
Marketing service publication
Office furniture, depreciation of
Office maintenance and rent
Premiums paid for acquisition of stock in short-sale transactions
Profit-sharing arrangements, payments in accordance with
Safe-deposit box rent
Secretary's salary
State stamp tax
Statistical services
Trustee's commission

Fig. B-4 (Page 1 of 2)

DEDUCTIBLE BUSINESS EXPENSES
Professional Persons and Merchants

Accounting fees

Advertising

Air raid shelter for employees

Appraisal costs (unless incurred in acquisition of property)

Attorney's fees, business—as for collecting accounts, etc.

Automobile upkeep, if used 50% or more in business

Bad debts

Chamber of Commerce dues, if membership used to advance business interests

Compensation paid, if reasonable

Computer software costs (purchased or leased)

Conventions, business, expenses of attending

Depreciation on furniture and fixtures

Education to maintain or improve skills

Fraternal organization dues for corporate officer if membership is for business
  purposes

Freight charges

Gifts for customers (limited to $25 per individual per year)

Insurance—fire, plate glass, holdup, burglary, group life, hospitalization, theft,
  public liability, storm, etc.

Interest (subject to limitations)

Investigation of prospective business (under certain conditions)

License fees

Light bills

Machinery—repairs and replacement of parts without prolonging life

Mortgage prepayment penalty

Night-watch service

Painting

Porter and janitor services

Postage

Refuse removal

Rent

Repairs to business property

Salaries, bonuses, commissions, etc., paid, excluding own salary if
  proprietorship

Fig. B-4 (Page 2 of 2)

Selling commissions
State legislator's travel expenses (if elected)
Stationery—letterheads, bills, envelopes, cards, etc.
Stock bought in settlement of dispute
Stock exchange fee to maintain listing of stock
Supplies—wrapping paper, boxes, twine, tape, signs, price tags, labels, etc.
Tax return, cost of preparing
Taxes
Telephone
Theft losses not compensated by insurance

Fig. B-5

DEDUCTIBLE AUTOMOBILE EXPENSES
Whether Auto is Used for Business or Pleasure

Interest on installment purchase payments, if carrying charges are stated (subject to limitations)

Interest on money borrowed in purchasing car (subject to limitations)

License fees

Loss and damage not compensated by insurance ($100 floor for pleasure cars), due to casualty (including collision), even though
- (a) due to faulty driving of taxpayer or other person operating automobile, if not due to willful negligence
- (b) caused by faulty driving of driver of car collided with

Loss and damage not compensated by insurance—due to fire, theft, or embezzlement

Fig. B-6

DEDUCTIBLE AUTOMOBILE EXPENSES
Only If Auto Is Used 50% or More for Business

Automobile club membership
Chauffeur's license and salary
Cost of automobile, if worn out within a year
Depreciation
Driver's license
Garage rental charges
Gasoline
Insurance
Judgment for damages due to negligent driving
License fees
Loss on sale of automobile
Lubrication
Oil
Parking
Repairs
Tires with life of less than one year
Washing

Fig. B-7

NONDEDUCTIBLE AUTOMOBILE EXPENSES

Accident damages paid, resulting from operation of pleasure car
Cost of automobile (unless business car is worn out within year)
Damage suit for negligent driving of pleasure car, expense of defending
Fines for violating traffic laws
Gasoline taxes, state
Loss on trade-in
Travel expenses between home and place of business

Fig. B-8

DEDUCTIBLE LOSSES

Abandonment
Automobile—damage from collision, damage from icy pavement or freezing
　　motor
Bombardment
Disaster losses
Drought
Earthquake
Experiments, unsuccessful
Fire
Flood
Forfeiture of part of purchase price (transaction for profit or business)
Gambling losses, to extent of gains only (if nonprofessional, these losses
　　deductible only from adjusted gross income)
Guaranty payments if in business or transaction entered into for profit or as bad
　　debts
Hedging transactions in commodity futures
Hurricane
Partner's sale of asset to partnership (with certain limitations)
Patent infringement, judgment paid for
Residence damaged by blasting; drought damage to foundations and footings;
　　fire; flood; sinking of land; water pipes freezing and bursting
Sale of property (if acquired or held for profit)
Shipwreck
Sonic-boom damages
Storm
Theft
Timber loss from fire, storm, etc.
Transactions entered into for profit though not connected with trade or business
Trees and shrubs damaged by storm or drought
Worthless securities (as capital loss)

Fig. B-9

NONDEDUCTIBLE LOSSES

Alimony not received
Anticipated income
Automobile trade-in, personal
Clothing damaged by moths
Commodity tax straddle losses (to the extent they do not exceed unrealized gains)
Excavation on adjacent property, damage to residence by
Family sales or exchange losses
Household goods damaged in storage or transit
Reduction in value
Residence, sale of property used exclusively as
Ring lost from owner's finger
Stock, decline in value of
Surrender of insurance policy
Termite damage
Transfer of property by gift or death
Trees, ornamental—destroyed by "Dutch elm" disease
Wash sales
Well drying up because of drought

OTHER NONDEDUCTIBLE EXPENSES

Adoption expense

Attorney's fees—breach of promise suit, contesting action for alimony arrearages, defending incompetency suit, establishing right to hold public office, negotiation of property settlements with wife, obtaining divorce, preparation of will, prosecuting a personal slander suit, tax advice to wife on property settlement where fee paid by husband to wife's attorney

Automobile upkeep expense—car used exclusively for pleasure

Bridge tolls

CPA review course

Checking fee on N.O.W. account

Child support payments

Clothing, personal

Commuting expenses

Damages paid for breach of promise to marry

Depreciation on property held for personal use and not for production of income

Diaper service (antiseptic)

Domestic servants (except as child care)

Dues—social club for personal use; officers' and noncommissioned officers' clubs

Employee's contribution to private disability fund in certain states

Employee's insurance, amount deducted from salary for

Fines for violation of law or police regulations

Fines paid by truckers for overweight or overlength trucks

Firefighter's meals and lodging on overnight duty at station

Food

Funeral expenses

Gifts, nonbusiness, to individuals

Hobby loss

House rent

Husband-to-wife allowance, paid as housewife's salary

Improper payments to officials of a foreign government

Insurance on residence

Life insurance premiums

Lobbying expenses (including expenditures to influence voters)

Loss on sale of club membership

Marriage counseling

Fig. B-10 (Page 2 of 2)

Maternity clothing
Medical, dental, and hospital expenses—less than 7.5% of adjusted gross
    income
Minor children, allowances to
Mortgage insurance premiums (FHA mortgage) paid by mortgagor (property not
    used in trade or business or held for production of income)
Political contributions, direct or indirect
Prepaid interest or finance charges (must be amortized over the life of the loan)
Raffle tickets
Reconditioning and health-restoring expenses paid by employees
Repairs to personal residence
Safe-deposit box rental for jewelry or personal effects
Singer's throat treatments (except as medical expenses)
Tax penalty payments
Transportation to and from place of employment of physically disabled
Traveling—in search of employment; no established residence
Unemployment compensation insurance premiums
Uniforms of military and naval officers, etc., which replace regular clothing
Wedding gifts to employees
Wife accompanying husband on business trip

Index

Edited by Carl H. Silverman